WORLD WAR II
HISTORY ILLUSTRATED IN
300 PHOTOS

Claudio Blanc

Camelot
EDITORA

President: Paulo Roberto Houch
MTB 0083982/SP

Editorial Coordination: Priscilla Sipans and Paola Houch
Art Coordination: Rubens Martim
Graphic Design: Renato Darim Parisotto
Image Selection: Claudio Blanc
Translation: Suellen Durães
English text review: Francine Oliveira
Images: Wikicommons
Sales: Phone: (11) 3393-7723 (vendas@editoraonline.com.br)

Legal deposit has been made.

International Data of Cataloging in Publication (CIP) according to ISBD

C181w — Camelot Editora

World War II: History illustrated in 300 photos/ Camelot Editora.– Barueri : Camelot Editora, 2024.
160 p. ; 15.1 x 23 in.

ISBN: 978-65-6095-131-0

1. Photography. I. Title.

2023-2188 — CDD 770 / CDU 77

Elaborated by Odilio Hilario Moreira Junior - CRB-8/9949

Rights reserved to
IBC – Instituto Brasileiro de Cultura LTDA
CNPJ 04.207.648/0001-94
Avenida Juruá, 762 — Alphaville Industrial
Zip Code: 06455-010 – Barueri/SP
www.editoraonline.com.br

1939 – PRELUDE

Italy invades Albania and annexes the country through a union with the Albanian crown.

... and the flag of the country under Italian rule.

The Pact of Steel, also known as the "Pact of Friendship and Alliance between Germany and Italy," was signed by Fascist Italy and Nazi Germany. The document declares cooperation between the two countries and establishes, in a secret annex, a military alliance.

Galeazzo Ciano, Adolf Hitler, and Joachim Von Ribbentrop at the signing of the Pact of Steel at the Reichskanzlei, the Reich Chancellery, in Berlin.

Einstein-Szilárd's letter was sent to the President of the United States, Franklin D. Roosevelt. Written by Leó Szilárd and signed by Albert Einstein, it warned about the risk of Germany developing atomic bombs. The document also recommended action on Roosevelt's part, and eventually resulted in the Manhattan Project.

The letter, conceived and written by Jewish-Hungarian physicist Leo Szilárd (below) and signed by Einstein, resulted in the creation of the Manhattan Project and the invention of the atomic bomb.

Leo Szilárd

The Molotov-Ribbentrop Pact, also known as the Mutual Non-Aggression Treaty, was signed between the Soviet Union and Nazi Germany. The document contained secret provisions on the division of Western Europe – the joint occupation of Poland and the Soviet occupation of the Baltics, Finland, and Bessarabia. The pact determined that there would be no Soviet intervention during the German invasion of Poland.

Stalin and Ribbentrop after the pact was signed.

Germany gives Poland an ultimatum demanding the Polish Corridor and the Free City of Danzig.

With no response to the ultimatum, Germany invades Poland, starting World War II.

September 1, 1939: Germans tear down Poland's border. World War II begins.

The Polish infantry in 1939.

A Polish soldier waiting
for the Nazis after Poland
failed to respond to the
German ultimatum.

The British Prime Minister
Neville Chamberlain and Hitler
in 1938.

THE WORLD WAR II

On September 1, 1939, the Nazis began their invasion of Poland. Two days later, Britain, France, Australia, and New Zealand declared war on Germany. The Nazis were not intimidated and continued their attack. The strategy used by the Germans, called Blitzkrieg (Lightning War), is based on a quick and surprise attack, and guaranteed the conquest of the territories of Denmark and Norway, capturing strategic ports. During the crisis, the Prime Minister of Great Britain, Neville Chamberlain, resigned from his position and was replaced by Winston Churchill on May 10, 1940. On the same day, Hitler's army invaded Luxembourg, Belgium, and the Netherlands.

Polish light tanks in formation during the early days of the Defensive War, 1939.

BATTLE OF MŁAWA | SEPTEMBER 1–3 |

This combat, in defense of the city of Mława, was one of the opening battles of the Invasion of Poland and the Second World War fought between the forces of Polish general Krukowicz-Przedrzymirski and German general Georg von Küchler.

BATTLE OF THE BZURA | SEPTEMBER 9–22 |

The Battle of Bzura, also known as the Battle of Kutno or the Battle of the Bzura River, was a Polish counterattack in response to the invasion of their country. Although the Polish forces were completely defeated, the attack delayed the Nazi advance and gave the Polish army some time to organize its defenses.

BATTLE OF TOMASZÓW LUBELSKI | SEPTEMBER 17–20 |

The Battle of Tomaszow Lubelski was the second major battle of the German campaign in Poland, resulting in a German victory.

Kazimiera Mika, a Polish girl, mourns the death of her older sister, Anna, shot in the open during a German air raid in Warsaw.

German infantry in street combat during the Polish campaign.

WAGNER/ GERMANY FEDERAL ARCHIVES

Shooting of Polish civilians by a German task force.

Prisoners of war murdered by the Nazis.

THE BATTLE OF WARSAW | SEPTEMBER 8–28 |

The Battle of Warsaw was the largest battle during the Nazi invasion of Poland. In addition to German and Polish troops, a small militia of civilian volunteers from Warsaw took part in the fighting. The occupation of Nazi Germany lasted until the city's liberation by the Allies on January 17, 1945.

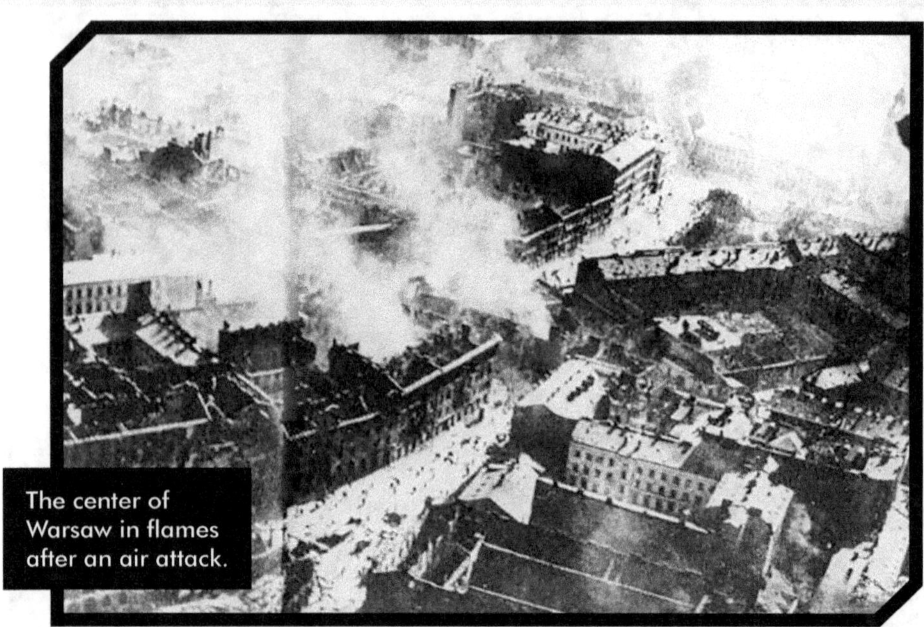

The center of Warsaw in flames after an air attack.

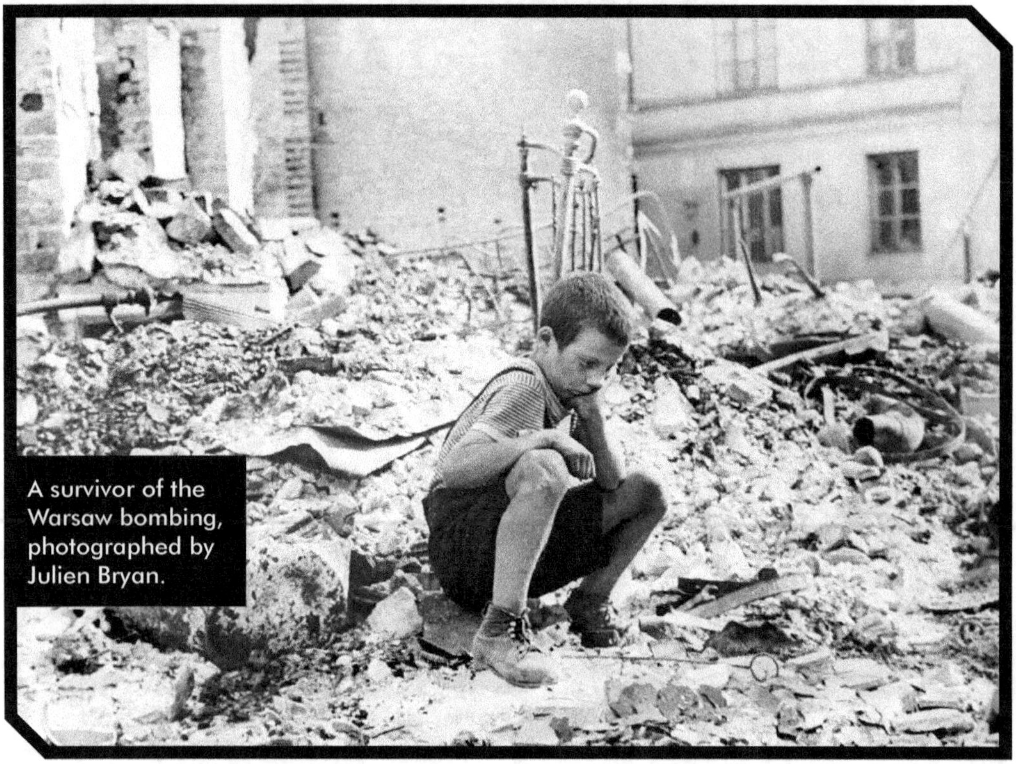

A survivor of the Warsaw bombing, photographed by Julien Bryan.

Civilian refugees in Warsaw.

Starving civilians try to obtain meat from the carcasses of dead horses.

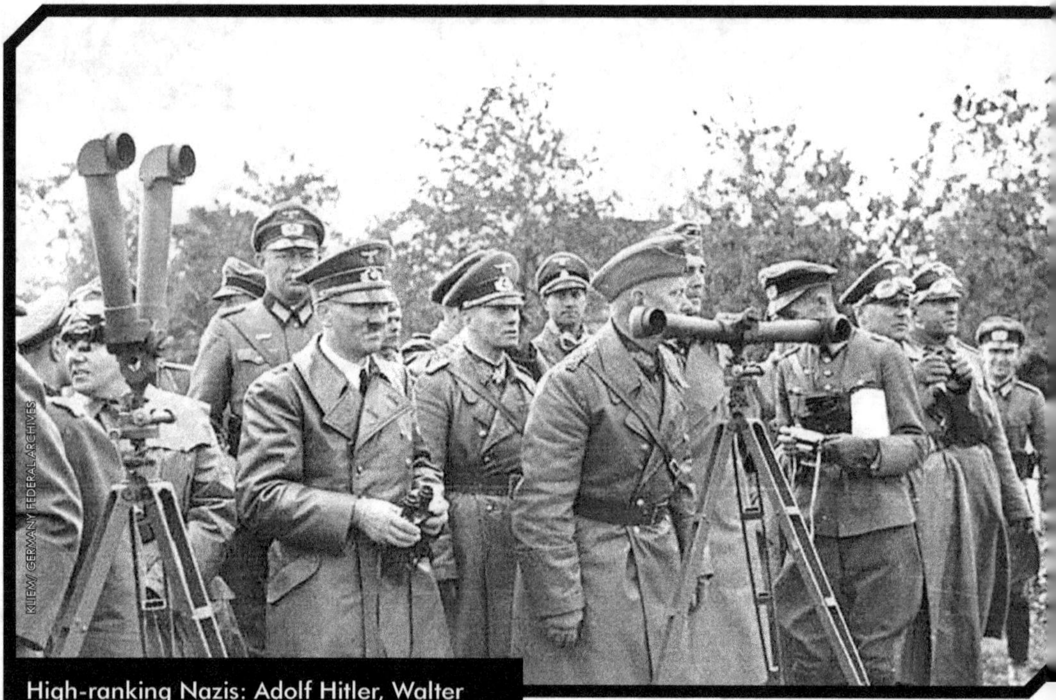
KLIEM/ GERMANY FEDERAL ARCHIVES

High-ranking Nazis: Adolf Hitler, Walter von Reichenau, Erwin Rommel, and Martin Bormann observing the siege of Warsaw.

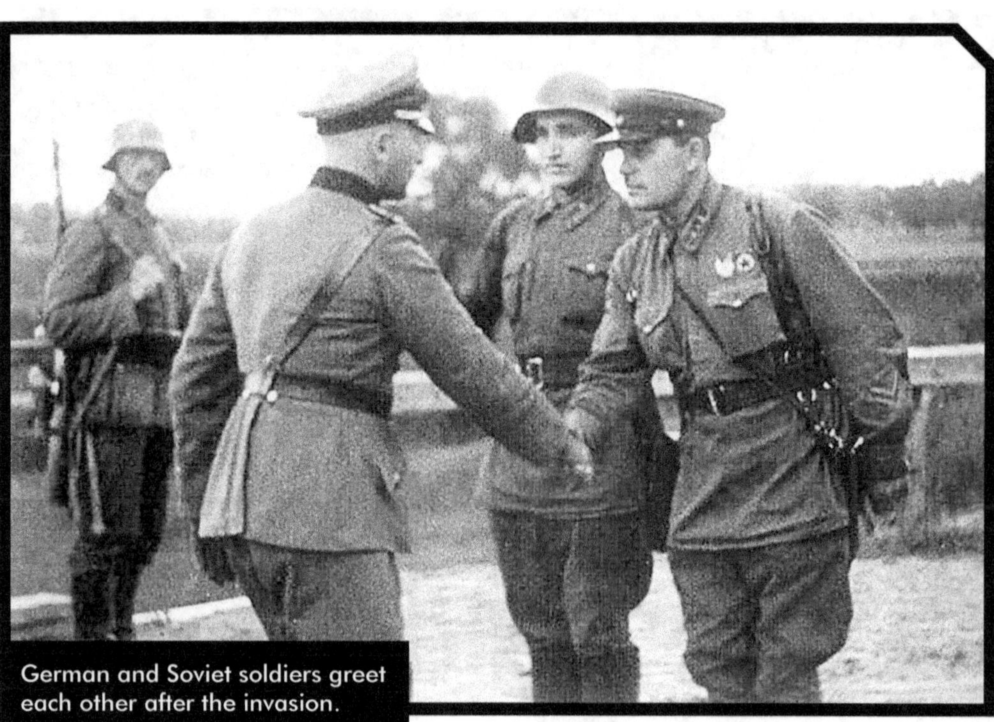

German and Soviet soldiers greet each other after the invasion.

BATTLE OF KOCK

OCTOBER 2–5

This was the final battle in the invasion of Poland, fought in the city that gave its name to the battle. It concluded the German invasion.

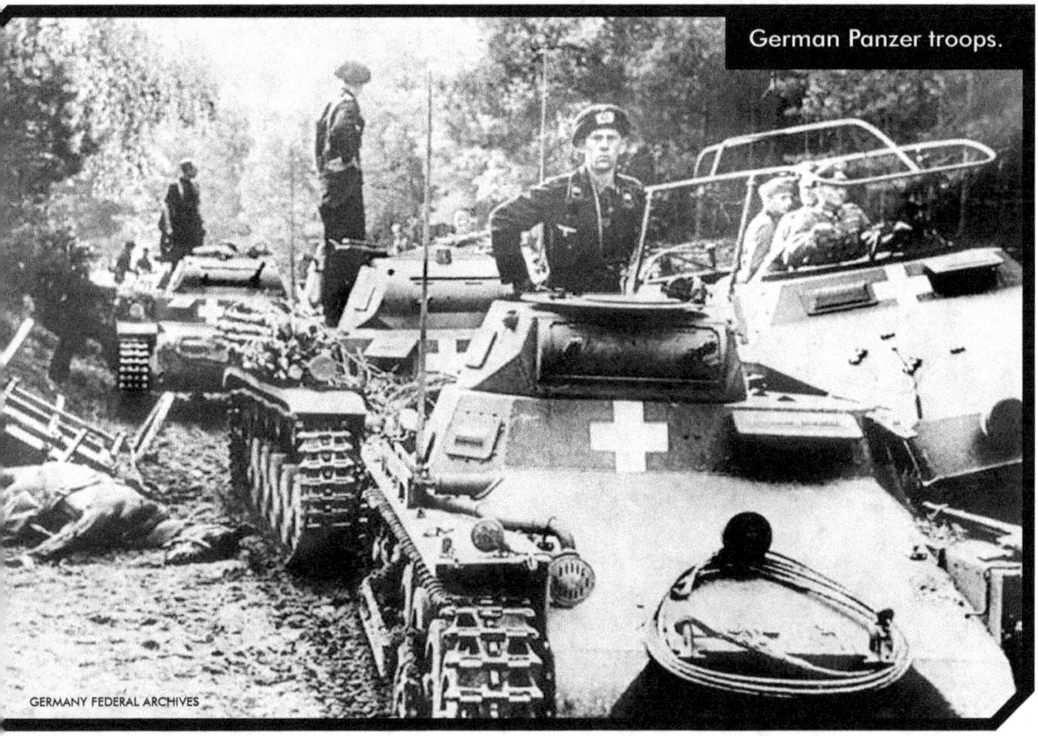
GERMANY FEDERAL ARCHIVES

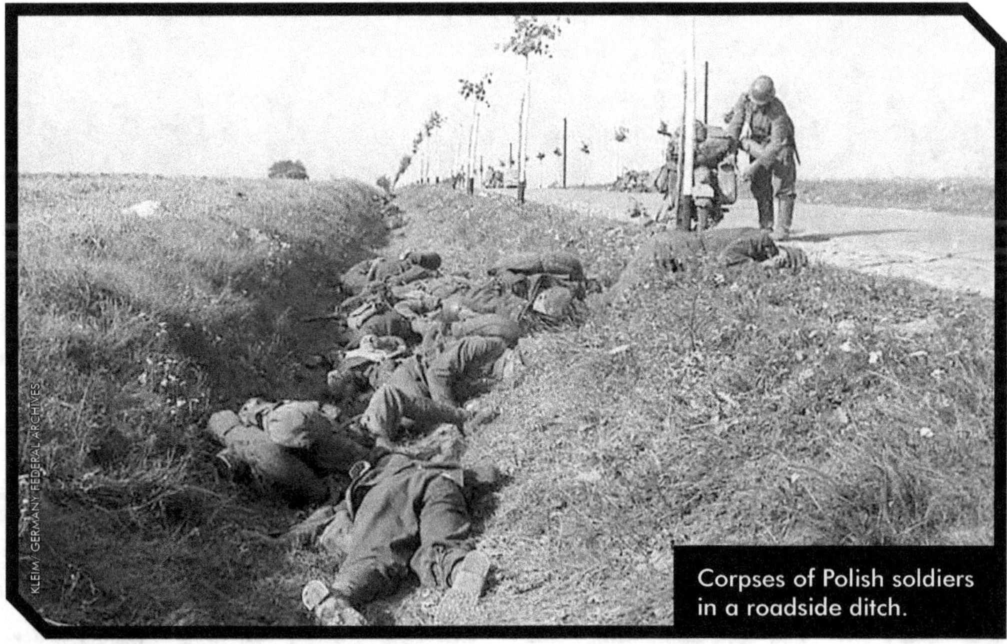

German Panzer troops.

KLEIM / GERMANY FEDERAL ARCHIVES

Corpses of Polish soldiers in a roadside ditch.

SAAR OFFENSIVE

| SEPTEMBER 7 – OCTOBER 16 |

The offensive was a French ground operation in Saarland, Germany, during the early stages of World War II. Although 30 divisions of the French army advanced to the border – and some even occupied a few cities and villages in the German state –, the invasion of the country was a failure. The quick victory in Poland allowed Germany to reorganize its army on the borders, halting the offensive. French forces withdrew amid a German counterattack on October 17.

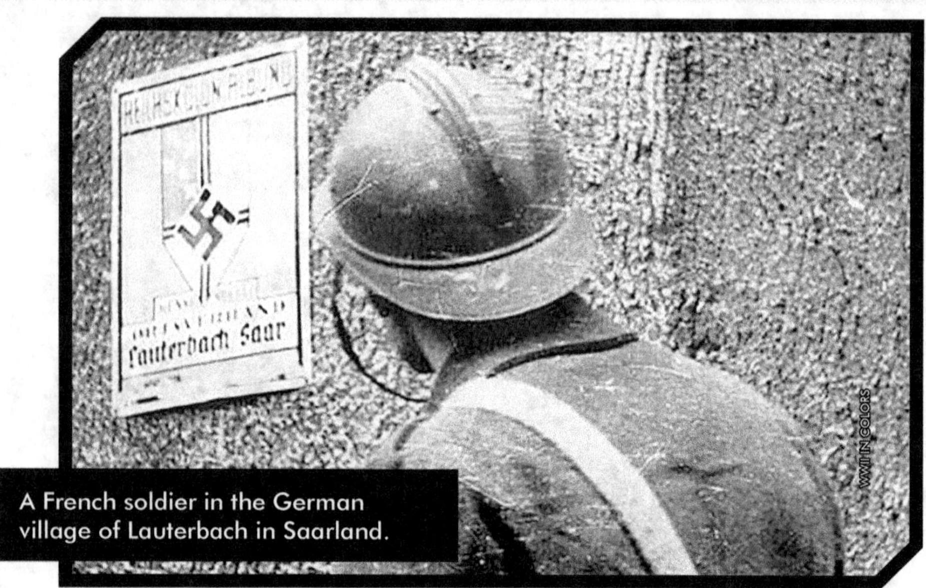

A French soldier in the German village of Lauterbach in Saarland.

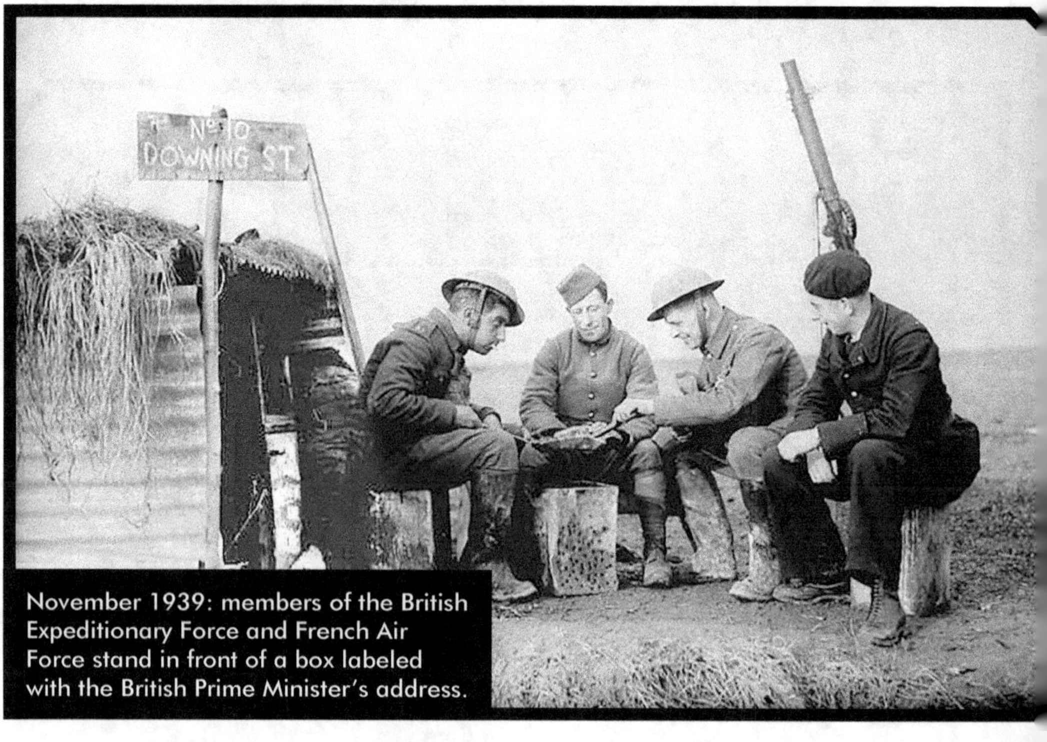

November 1939: members of the British Expeditionary Force and French Air Force stand in front of a box labeled with the British Prime Minister's address.

1940

BATTLE OF THE ATLANTIC | SEPTEMBER 3, 1939 – MAY 8, 1945 |

The battle was a landmark in World War II. Fought between the Axis powers and the Allies, the confrontation was aimed, on the part of the Nazis, at blocking the Allied sea routes in the Atlantic, seeking to prevent the arrival of supplies to the United Kingdom and the Soviet Union and also the arrival of American troops in the European Theater of Operations.

Depth charges detonate in the stern of HMS Starling, responsible for the sinking of 14 U-boats during the war.

Hedgehog: anti-submarine mortar installed in the bow of the destroyer HMS Westcott.

A submarine fires on a merchant ship that remained afloat after being torpedoed.

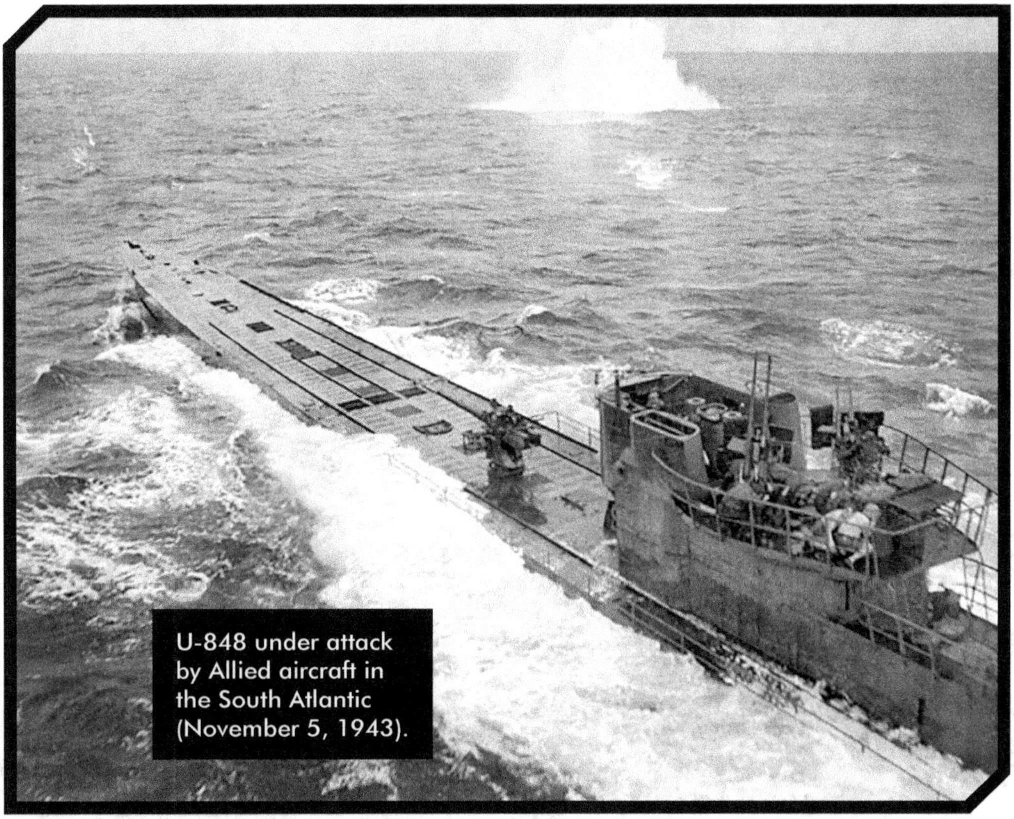

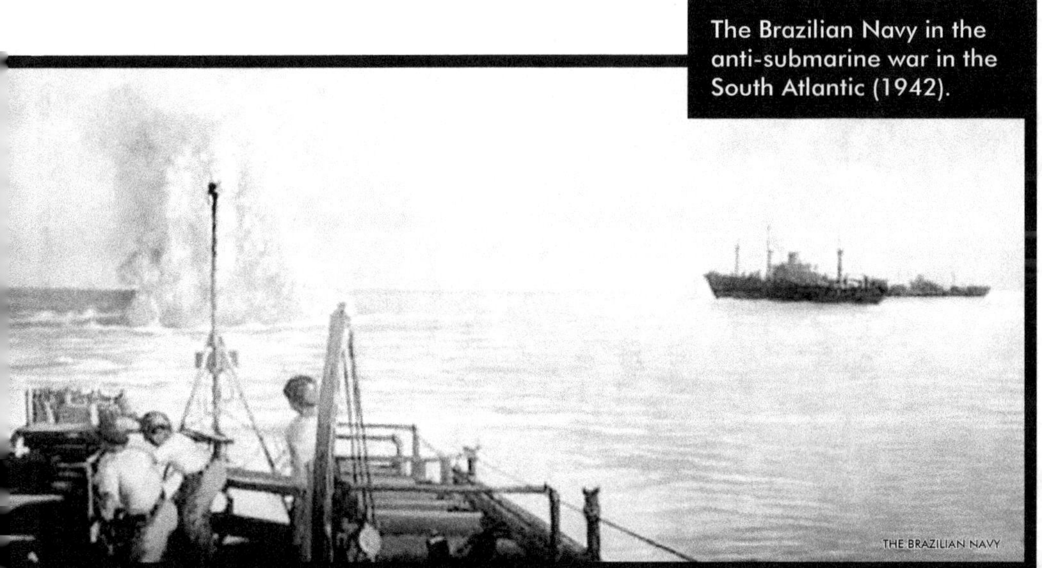

U-848 under attack by Allied aircraft in the South Atlantic (November 5, 1943).

The Brazilian Navy in the anti-submarine war in the South Atlantic (1942).

THE BRAZILIAN NAVY

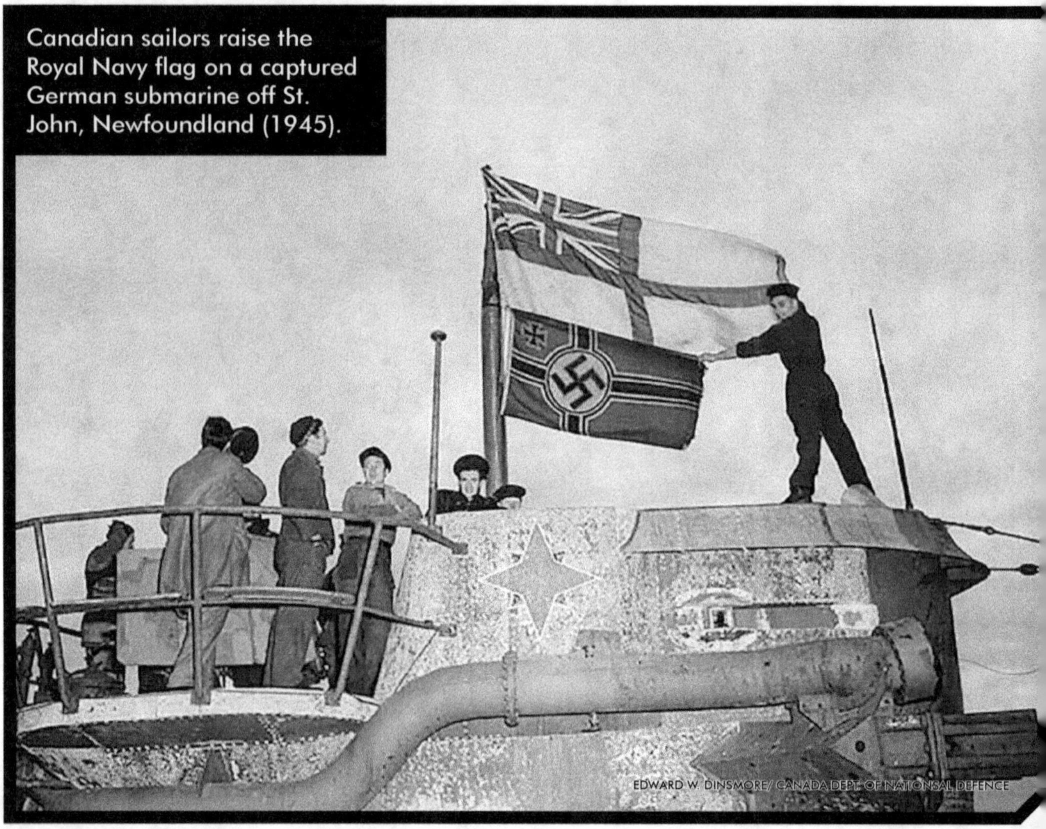

Canadian sailors raise the Royal Navy flag on a captured German submarine off St. John, Newfoundland (1945).

EDWARD W. DINSMORE/ CANADA DEPT. OF NATIONAL DEFENCE

The Wake Island, a Casablanca-class escort ship.

BATTLE OF THE NETHERLANDS | MAY 10–14 |

The Battle of the Netherlands was the German invasion of the region of the Netherlands comprising Belgium, Luxembourg, and the Netherlands. The battle took place simultaneously with the invasion of France and ended shortly after the bombing of Rotterdam by the Luftwaffe. The Netherlands remained under Nazi occupation until 1945.

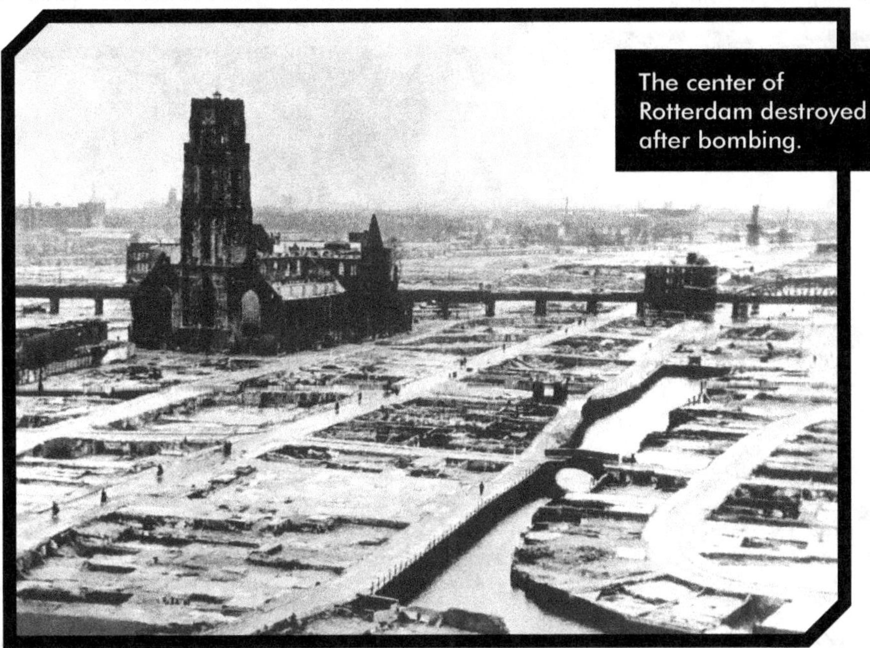

The center of Rotterdam destroyed after bombing.

H. LAMME/ NATIONAAL ARCHIEF

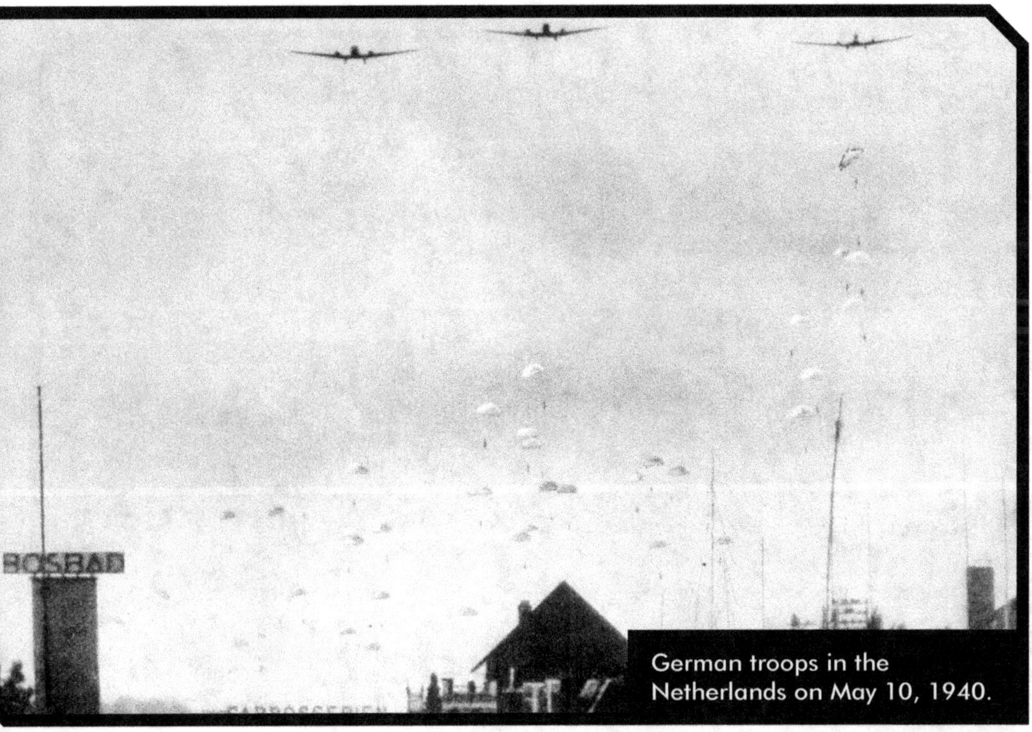

German troops in the Netherlands on May 10, 1940.

BATTLE OF BELGIUM | MAY 10–29 |

Also known as the Belgian Campaign or the 18 Days Campaign, it was part of the Battle of France. With this operation, Germany defeated and occupied Belgium according to the Case Yellow (Fall Gelb). There were 18 days of heavy fighting and the Belgian army was a great opponent for the German troops. Belgium's defeat forced the Allies to withdraw from the European continent.

Belgian soldiers under German guard after the fall of Fort Eben-Emael (May 11, 1940).

RA BOE/WIKIPEDIA

German soldiers seize Belgian weapons in Bruges after the surrender.

V. HAUSEN / GERMANY FEDERAL ARCHIVES

BATTLE OF FRANCE

The Battle of France, or the Fall of France, was the result of the Nazi invasion of French territory. German armored units outflanked the Maginot Line and defeated the Allied troops. The British Expeditionary Force was evacuated from Dunkirk in what became known as Operation Dynamo, and many French units joined the Resistance or sided with the Allies.

Men of the 1st Royal Welch Fusiliers (Wales) near Etaples (February 1940).

War refugees on a French road.

BATTLE OF DUNKIRK | MAY 25 – JUNE 4 |

During this confrontation, large British and French forces were trapped by a German panzer division northeast of France, between the Calais coastal channel. More than 300,000 Allied soldiers were evacuated by sea. At this moment, which would be one of the most memorable of the war, even civilian vessels were used to remove soldiers from the beaches of Dunkirk. Had it not been for the fact that they were separated from the continent by sea, the countries of Great Britain would have been compromised, and the war could have had a different outcome.

A British soldier in Dunkirk fires at German planes.

BATTLE OF BRITAIN | JULY 10 – OCTOBER 31 |

After the withdrawal of British troops from Dunkirk, Hitler began a series of bombing raids against Great Britain. In a massive area, the German Air Force attacked bases of the British Royal Air Force, the RAF. By September 1940, the Germans believed they had completely destroyed the RAF and began the Blitz, as the series of bombings over London was called. However, the British resisted until the Nazis stopped the Blitz in May 1941.

A Spitfire pilot tells how he shot down a Messerschmitt (September 1940).

A member of the
London Fire Service:
after the bombings,
the fires spread.

1941

BARBAROSSA OPERATION

Operation Barbarossa was the code name for the Nazi invasion of the Soviet Union that began on June 22, 1941. Throughout the action, around four million Axis soldiers invaded the Soviet borders, forming a front of 1,800 miles – the largest invasion force in history. In addition to the large number of soldiers, the Germans also used 600,000 vehicles and around 700,000 horses in this effort. The operation was motivated by Hitler's ideological desire to conquer Soviet territories, as he had established in his book Mein Kampf. The invasion marked the rapid intensification of the war and resulted in the Soviet Union forming a coalition with the Allied countries. Many critics claim that Operation Barbarossa was Hitler's biggest mistake.

German soldiers armed with flamethrowers in the Soviet Union.

Belarusian children during a Nazi air raid (June, 24 1941).

A German soldier with a flamethrower.

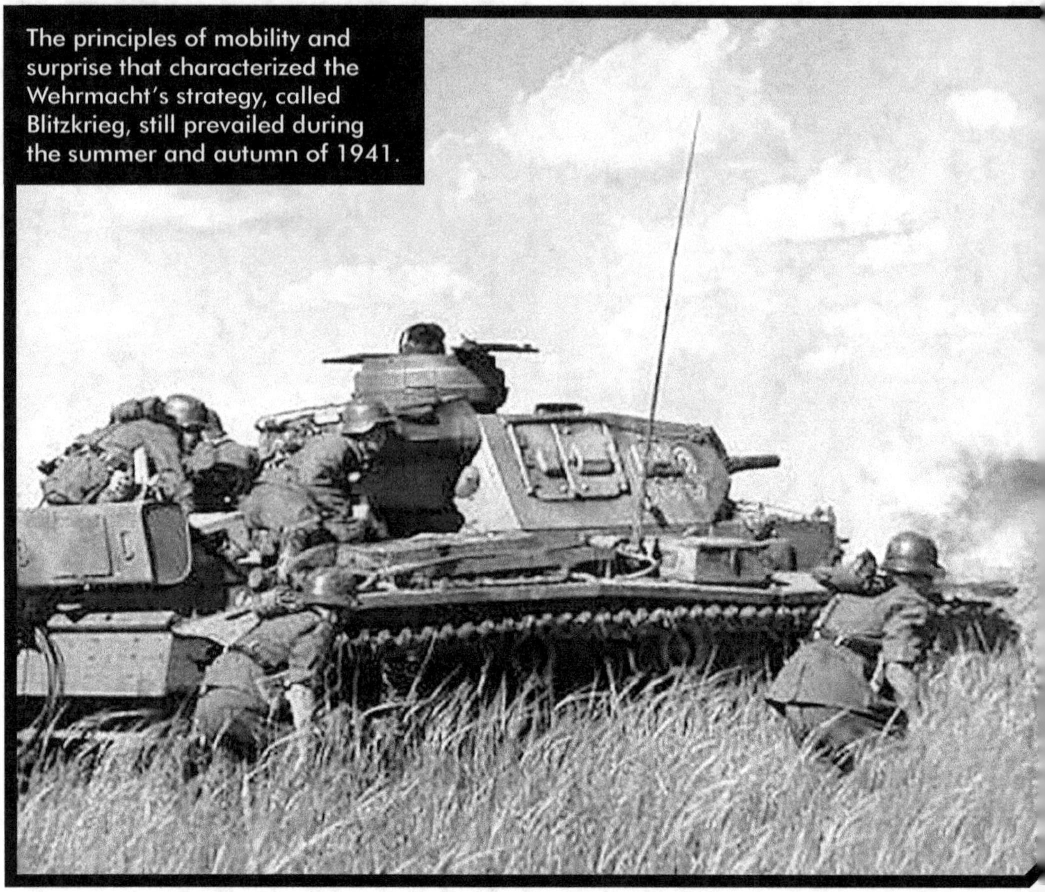

The principles of mobility and surprise that characterized the Wehrmacht's strategy, called Blitzkrieg, still prevailed during the summer and autumn of 1941.

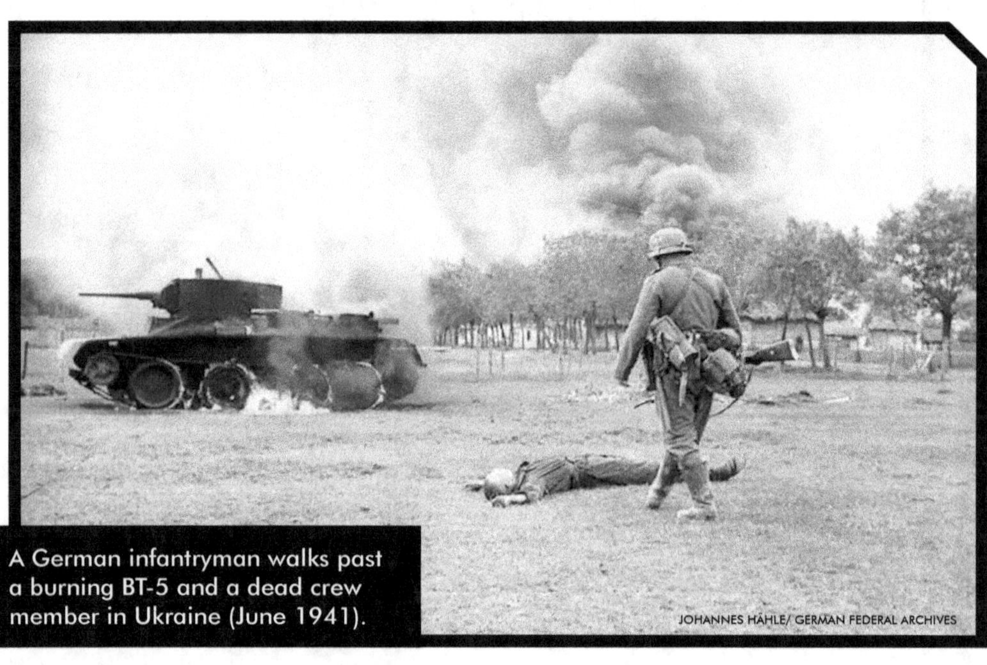

A German infantryman walks past a burning BT-5 and a dead crew member in Ukraine (June 1941).

JOHANNES HÄHLE/ GERMAN FEDERAL ARCHIVES

Soviet planes fly over German positions near Moscow.

BATTLE OF SMOLENSK

| JULY 6 – AUGUST 5 |

The battle for the city of Smolensk, halfway to Moscow, concluded the conquest of Belarus. The operation ended in German victory.

Red Army soldiers near Smolensk.

Soviet soldiers fighting
at Dorogobuzh
(September 1, 1941).

BATTLE OF KYIV | AUGUST 23 – SEPTEMBER 26 |

The Battle of Kyiv was an operation that launched a large siege of Soviet troops on the outskirts of Kyiv. It was the largest troop siege in history, with almost the entire Southwestern Front of the Red Army surrounded by the Germans – around 665,000 soldiers. However, small groups of Red Army troops managed to escape. The Battle of Kyiv was an unprecedented defeat for the Red Army.

Kyiv after the bombings.

One of the Wehrmacht positions in Kyiv, captured the day before.

BATTLE OF MOSCOW | SEPTEMBER 30, 1941 – APRIL 20, 1942 |

The Battle of Moscow took place along a 373-mile line between October 1941 and January 1942. The Soviet defensive effort thwarted the Nazi attack on the nation's capital, one of the main military and basic political objectives of the Axis Forces.

December 1941: newly called up Soviet forces go to the Moscow front.

With all men at the front, women dig anti-tank trenches around Moscow.

A stamp shows a parade of Soviet troops on the Red Square on November 7, 1941.

STAMP OF MARTYNOV I./ PAINTING BY K. F. YUON

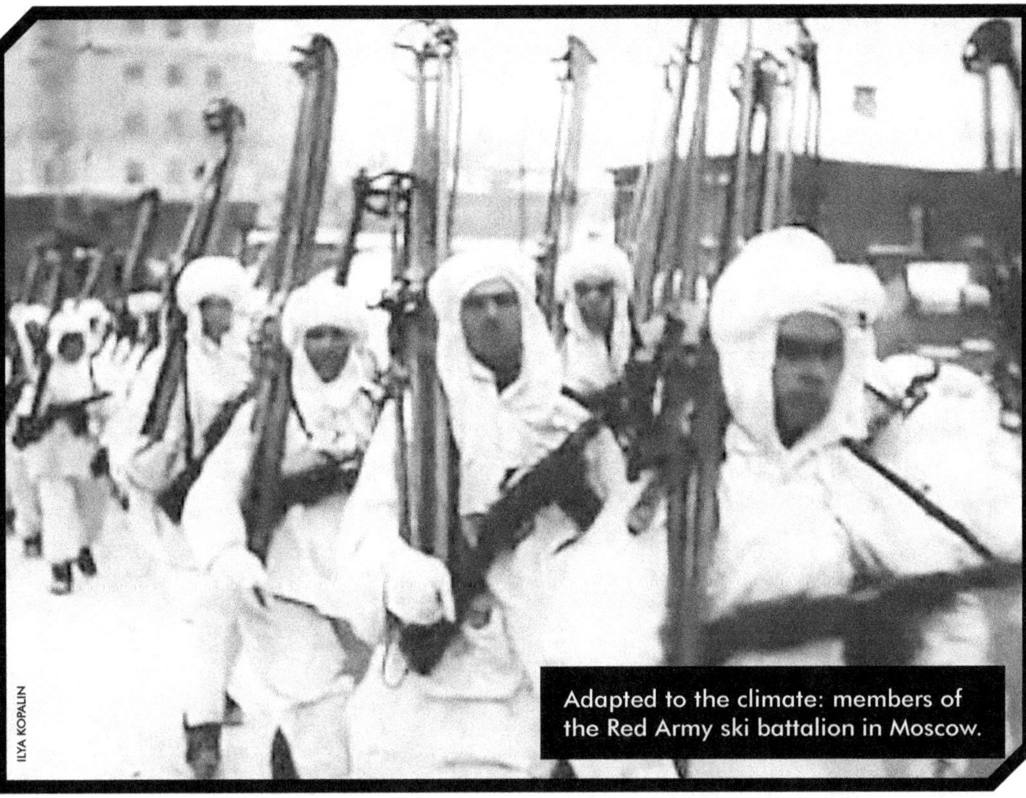

ILYA KOPALIN

Adapted to the climate: members of the Red Army ski battalion in Moscow.

A soviet machine gun nest attacking German infantry near Tulum (in November 1941).

ATACK ON PEARL HARBOR | DECEMBER 7 |

Until the end of 1941, despite not being at war, the United States collaborated by providing financial aid and supplies in the effort against the Axis. When Japan invaded northern Indochina, the United States boycotted the Japanese, cutting off supplies. The Japanese had no alternative but to fight those who blocked their expansion plans. On December 7, 1941, a Japanese task force attacked the United States Pacific Fleet, stationed at Pearl Harbor, Hawaii. The event launched the US into the war.

A photograph of the Battle Line taken from the Japanese fleet, at the beginning of the attack; two Japanese planes can be seen in full attack.

Pearl Harbor seen from the southwest side of the base.

The USS Arizona explodes.

Explosion of the destroyer USS Shaw, another of the American warships that were sunk in the attack.

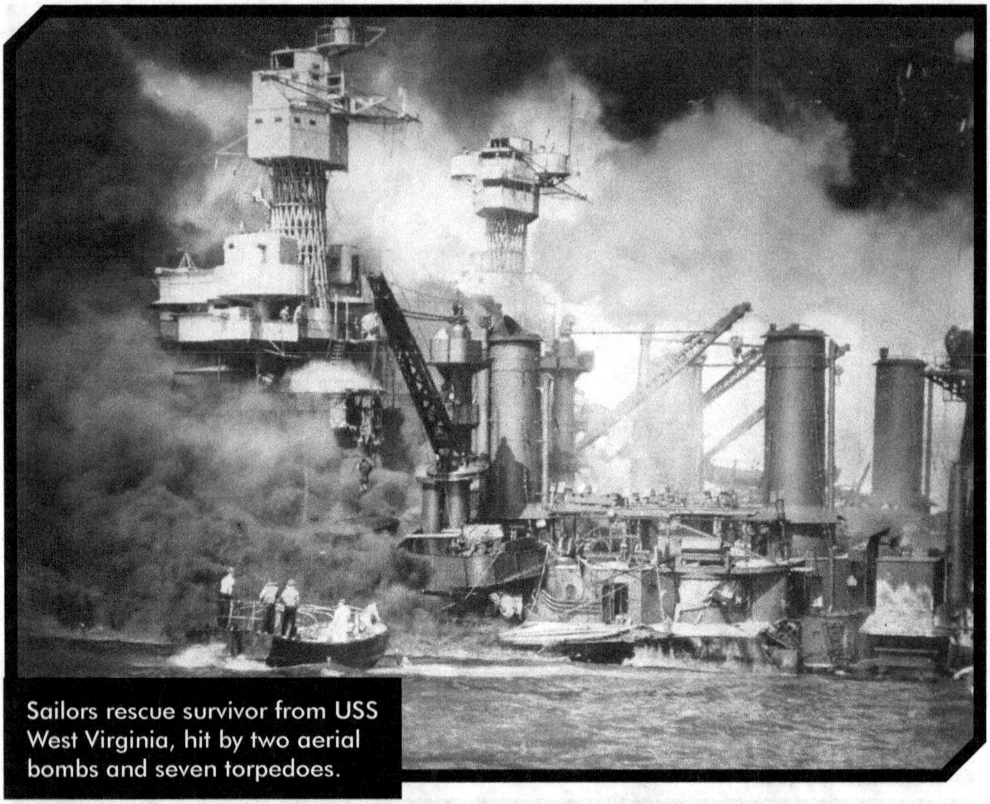

Sailors rescue survivor from USS West Virginia, hit by two aerial bombs and seven torpedoes.

BATTLE OF THAILAND

DECEMBER 8

Despite fierce resistance in the southern region of the country, the Japanese took just one day to invade and occupy Thailand.

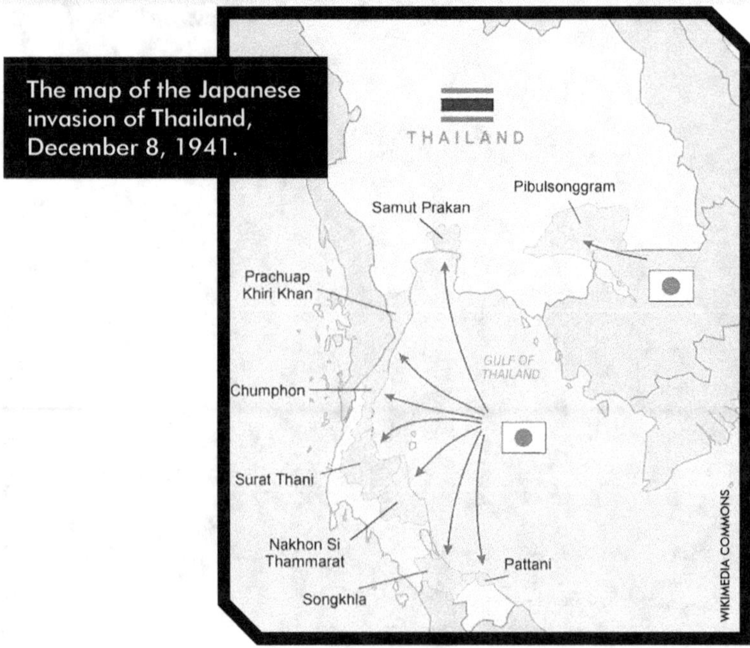

The map of the Japanese invasion of Thailand, December 8, 1941.

BATTLE OF HONG KONG | DECEMBER 8 – 25 |

Also referred to as the Fall of Hong Kong, it was one of the first battles of the Pacific War, beginning on the same day as the attack on the United States naval base at Pearl Harbor. Hong Kong was then a possession of the British Empire. As Japan had not declared war against the British, the attack violated international law. Less than two weeks after the start of operations, with the position on the island untenable, the British colony surrendered to the Japanese.

Japanese artillery in action in Hong Kong.

Canadian reinforcements in Hong Kong: carabinieri battalions (Rifle Battalion) known as "C Force".

The Japanese cross the Shenzhen River, which borders Hong Kong.

The Japanese victory parade in Hong Kong, 1941.

FIRST BATTLE OF GUAM

Fought during the War of the Pacific in the Mariana Islands, it resulted in the defeat of the American garrison on the island by Japanese forces. The Japanese occupied the base and remained there until the Second Battle of Guam in 1944.

An SB2U Vindicator on anti-submarine patrol (27 November 1941).

Natives of the Chamorro ethnic group on the Japanese-occupied island Saipan.

BATTLE OF WAKE ISLAND

The Battle of Wake Island was a Japanese invasion that occurred simultaneously with other attacks against the United States, including the attack on Pearl Harbor. Japan took control of the island on December 23, after two weeks of fighting, when the Americans surrendered.

The carcass of a Wildcat 211-F-11 piloted by Captain Henry T. Elrod in the attack that sank the Japanese destroyer Kisaragi on December 8.

MALAYSIAN CAMPAIGN | DECEMBER 8, 1941 – JANUARY 31, 1942 |

The Malayan Campaign was the confrontation of Allied and Axis forces in British Malaya. Operations were dominated by land battles, with minor skirmishes early in the action. For the British, Indian, Australian, and Malay forces who defended the colony, the campaign was an unmitigated disaster. The battle is notable for the Japanese use of cycling troops, which allowed soldiers to carry more equipment and move more quickly through dense forest terrain.

Royal Engineers preparing to blow up a bridge near Kuala Lumpur during the withdrawal.

1942

The Battle of Singapore was a siege of this island city-state. For almost two weeks, the besieged resisted the Japanese attacks as best they could, trying to sabotage and destroy the main structures that the enemies could take advantage of, and finally, they surrendered.

Commander Yamashita (seated in the center) pounds the table with his fist to emphasize his terms – unconditional surrender. The British leader, Percival, among his officers, holds his closed hand to his mouth.

Japanese soldiers shooting blindfolded Indian prisoners of the Sikh religion.

BATTLE OF THE JAVA SEA | FEBRUARY 27 |

In this battle, which took place at the beginning of the Pacific War, the Allies suffered a major defeat off the coasts of Indonesia and New Guinea, on February 27 and which, in the days that followed, broke up into smaller battles, such as the Battle of the Sunda Strait, which made this the largest surface naval battle to have occurred since the First World War.

A Japanese plane attacking the Dutch ship Java, during the Battle of the Java Sea.

The Japanese cruiser Haguro, which sank the HNLMS De Ruyter, killing Admiral Karel Doorman.

BATTLE OF BADUNG STRAIT
NIGHT OF THE 19ᵀᴴ AND EARLY MORNING OF THE 20ᵀᴴ OF FEBRUARY

The Battle of Badung Strait was fought by Allied ships and the Imperial Japanese Navy. The confrontation demonstrated the considerable superiority of the Japanese navy.

The HNLMS Ruyter shortly before being sunk in the Battle of the Java Sea. The Ruyter was later sunk, losing 344 of its crew.

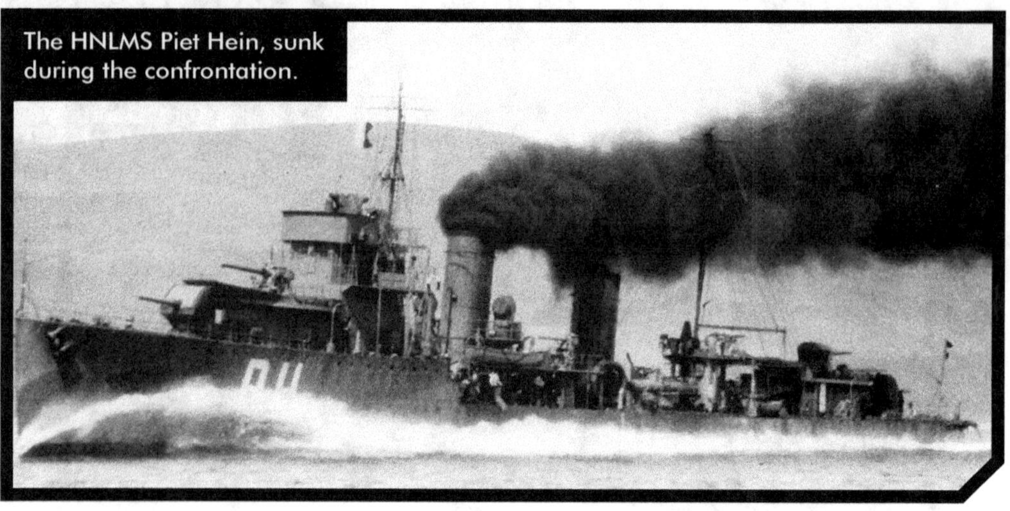

The HNLMS Piet Hein, sunk during the confrontation.

BATTLE OF JAVA | FEBRUARY 8 – MARCH 12 |

Also called the Invasion of Java, the battle took place on this island between the Empire of Japan and the Allies. At the end of the confrontation, a final surrender was signed by the Allied commanders.

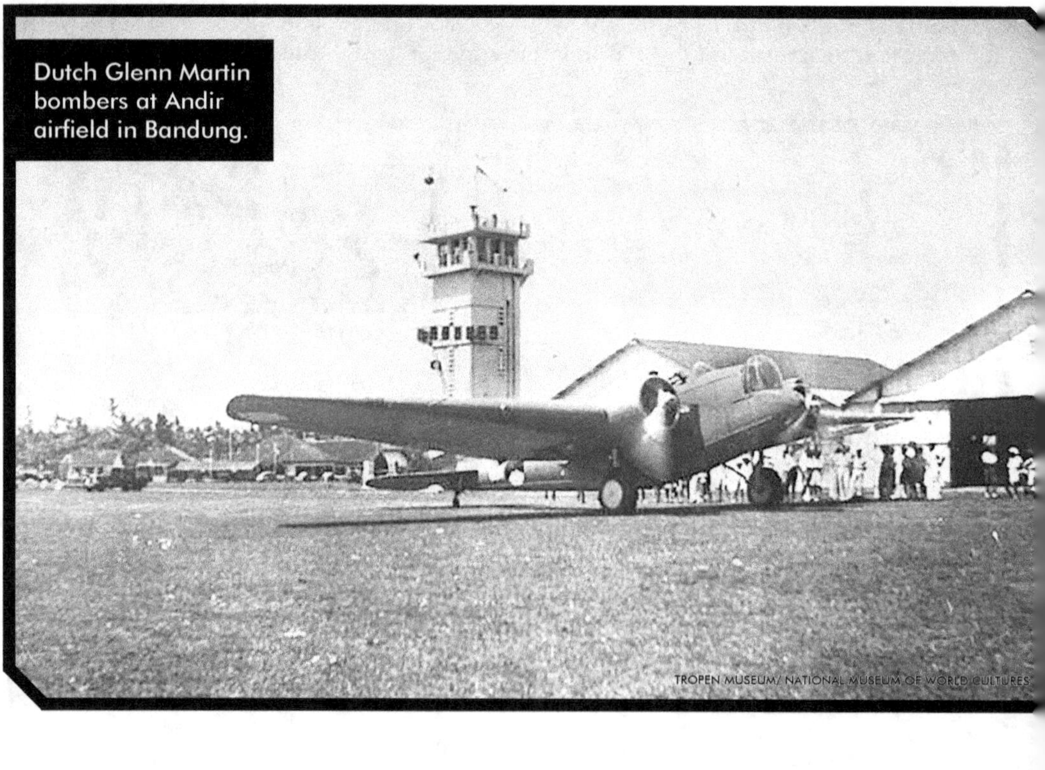
Dutch Glenn Martin bombers at Andir airfield in Bandung.

TROPEN MUSEUM/ NATIONAL MUSEUM OF WORLD CULTURES

BATTLE OF CORREGIDOR | MAY 5 – 6 |

The Battle of Corregidor was the culmination of Japan's military campaign, ensuring the country's conquest of the Philippines. With the fall of Bataan, the fort on Corregidor Island, located at the entrance to Manila Bay, the capital of the Philippines, was the last bastion of the Allied defense against the Japanese invasion of the country. However, the Allied defenses did not resist and the battle became one of the USA's worst military defeats.

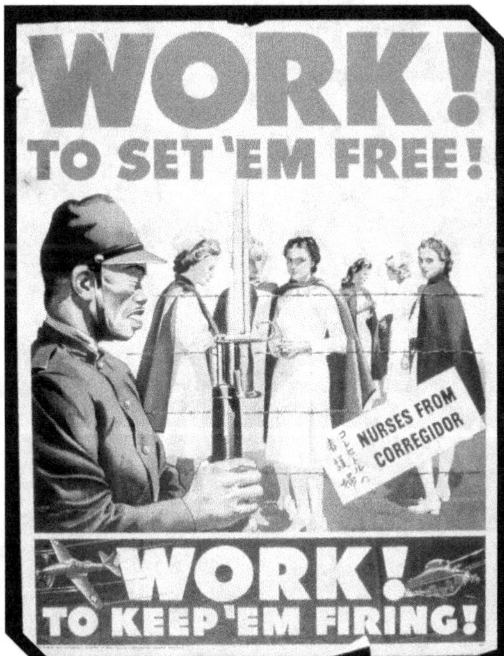

A poster for the American campaign to rescue prisoner nurses on Corregidor; the Japanese soldier is portrayed with caricatured features.

JAPANESE CONQUEST OF BURMA | 1942 – 1945 |

The Japanese conquest of Burma was a chapter in the Southeast Asian Campaign that stretched over four years, between 1942 and 1945. During the first year of the campaign, the Japanese army expelled British and Chinese forces from Burma, occupying the country and establishing a nominally independent Burmese administrative government.

The 15th Army on the Burma border.

Electrical and oil installations in Yenangyaung being destroyed as part of the "scorched earth" policy in the face of the Japanese advance.

Oil wells near Yenangyaung.

Troops of the Japanese 55th Division in Pegu.

Chinese leader Chiang Kai-shek with General Stilwell in Maymyo.

General Joseph Stilwell, his staff, and a smaller escort as they cross a river during the retreat to British India, early May 1942.

In June 1942, the Japanese attempted to invade Hawaii, but the plan was intercepted by the Americans, who destroyed a large part of the Japanese fleet in the Battle of Midway, considered the most important naval confrontation of the Pacific War. After this victory, the Americans sought to recapture several islands in the Pacific.

A Japanese aircraft carrier maneuvers to avoid bombs dropped by Boeing B-17 bombers.

Sailor George Gay (right), sole survivor of the TBD Devastator squadron.

Yorktown at the moment of a torpedo impact from a B5N Nakajima.

The aircraft carrier Hiryu just before sinking.

The Mikuma just before sinking.

Hiryu survivors.

BATTLE OF EL ALAMEIN

The First Battle of El Alamein was fought by Nazi forces commanded by General Erwin Rommel and British forces commanded by Claude Auchinleck. The confrontation concluded with the Allies' first important victory in Africa.

The British Army in North Africa: infantry in a defensive position near El Alamein.

The Afrika Korps on the move, with an Sd.Kfz.232 armored car leading the way.

Rommel in Africa, June 1942.

The Royal Australian Artillery at El Alamein (July 12, 1942).

The Panzer II Division of the Afrika Korps.

DÖRNER/ GERMAN FEDERAL ARCHIVES

Field Marshal Erwin Rommel with his aides during the desert campaign.

A soldier inspects a stricken Italian M13/40 tank near El Alamein.

The Royal Artillery in action.

SECOND BATTLE OF EL ALAMEIN
| OCTOBER 23 – NOVEMBER 11 |

The second Battle of El Alamein was the beginning of the defeat of the Axis forces in North Africa. After the British victory at El Alamein, Prime Minister Winston Churchill stated that "this is not the end, it is not even the beginning of the end, but it is, perhaps, the end of the beginning." After the war, Churchill wrote: "Before Alamein, we never had a victory, after Alamein we never had a defeat."

British infantry advances through the dust and smoke of battle.

Erwin Rommel (left) in command of Nazi operations.

British artillery barrage at the opening of the second battle of El Alamein.

A mine explodes near a British artillery truck in a minefield.

British tanks advance after infantry opened gaps in the enemy minefield at El Alamein (October 24, 1942).

A British soldier makes an obscene gesture to German prisoners captured at El Alamein (October 26, 1942).

Tanks of 8th Armored Brigade waiting to enter battle (October 27, 1942).

German prisoners.

A German 88mm gun abandoned near the coast road west of El Alamein (November 7, 1942).

BATTLE OF SEVASTOPOL | OCTOBER 30, 1941 – JULY 4, 1942 |

The Siege of Sevastopol resulted from the Wehrmacht's objective of controlling the Sevastopol base on the Black Sea. The Germans, commanded by Erich von Manstein, won the battle.

Motoscafo Armato Silurante (MAS), a camouflaged boat of the Italian Navy.

Torpedo training exercise in the Black Sea.

The port of Sevastopol after the battle.

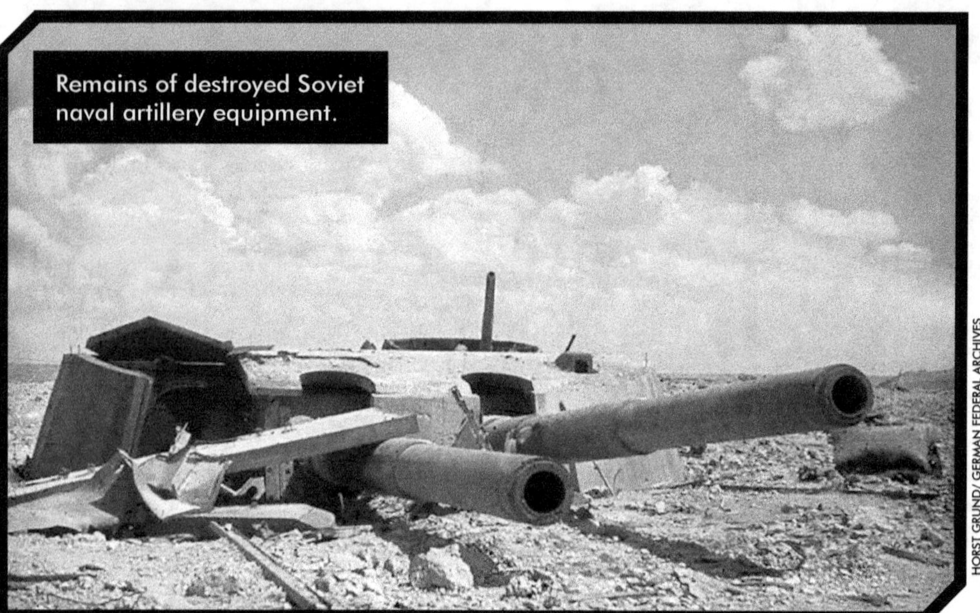

Remains of destroyed Soviet naval artillery equipment.

HORST GRUND/ GERMAN FEDERAL ARCHIVES

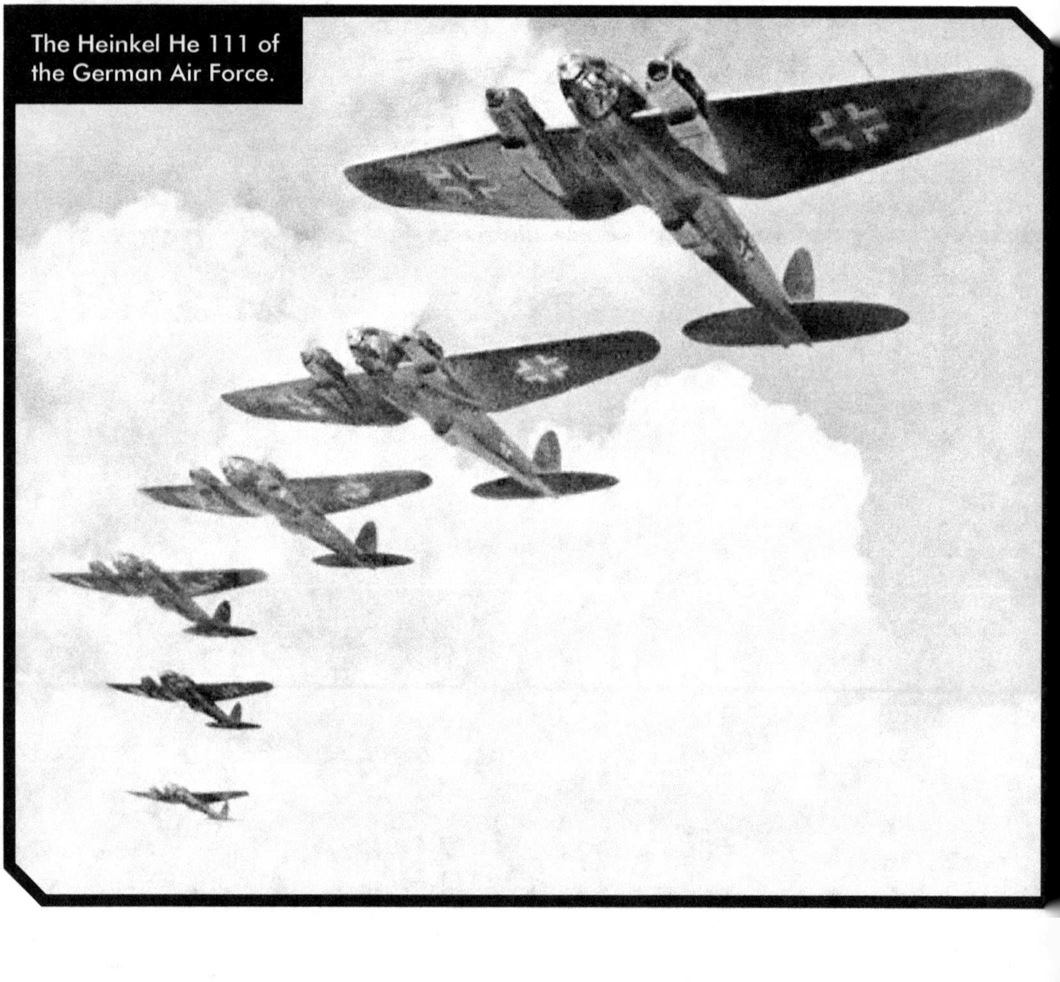

The Heinkel He 111 of the German Air Force.

The port of Sevastopol during the war.

KOKODA CAMPAIGN | JULY 21 – NOVEMBER 6 |

The Kokoda Trail Campaign consisted of a series of battles in the period from July to November 1942 between Japanese and Allied troops and, mainly, Australian forces in the then-Australian territory of Papua.

Australian soldiers of the 39th Battalion (September 1942).

American General MacArthur with General Sir Thomas Blamey and Prime Minister Curtin in a conference on campaign operations.

Native porters known as the "Fuzzy Wuzzy Angels" transport a wounded Australian soldier on a stretcher through the tropical jungle (August 30, 1942).

Members of the 39th Battalion in retreat after the Battle of Isurava.

Allied commanders in New Guinea in October 1942. From left to right: Mr. Frank Forde (Australian Minister for the Army); General Douglas MacArthur; General Sir Thomas Blamey; Lieutenant general George C. Kenney; Lieutenant General Edmund Herring; and Brigadier General Kenneth Walker.

An Australian soldier inspects abandoned Japanese artillery ammunition at Ioribaiwa.

A C-47 transport plane dropping supplies for the Australian 25th Brigade near the village of Nauru (October 1942).

BATTLE OF GUADALCANAL | AUGUST 1942 – FEBRUARY 1943 |

The Battle of Guadalcanal, or Guadalcanal Campaign, was fought on land, air, and sea by Americans, Australians, and Japanese on the island of Guadalcanal, in the Solomon Islands archipelago. It was the first major offensive undertaken by the Allies in the Pacific War after the attack on Pearl Harbor and the Battle of Midway, and the first Allied victory on land in the Pacific War.

The airport at Lunga Point on Guadalcanal was built by the Japanese with Korean workers.

American marines land on Guadalcanal (August 7, 1942).

Japanese soldiers killed on Guadalcanal after the Battle of the Tenaru.

The USS Enterprise (CV-6) under air attack during combat in the Solomon Islands.

Japanese troops board the "Tokyo Express" for Guadalcanal.

The Lieutenant Colonel Merritt A. Edson led Marine forces at the Battle of Edson's Ridge.

An American Navy patrol crosses the Matanikau River in September 1942.

Allied commanders gathered on Guadalcanal, in August 1943, to plan the next Allied offensive against the Japanese in the Solomon Islands as part of Operation Cartwheel.

BATTLE OF STALINGRAD
| JULY 17, 1942 – FEBRUARY 2, 1943 |

In the spring of 1942, Hitler ordered the siege of Stalingrad, one of the most dramatic moments of the war. The battle was marked by extreme brutality and disregard for military and civilian losses on both sides, the German offensive on the city of Stalingrad, the fighting within the city, and the Soviet counteroffensive that destroyed the entire German 6th Army and other Axis forces. In early 1943, the Soviets won the Battle of Stalingrad, and Nazi Germany was beginning to crumble.

HERBER/ GERMAN FEDERAL ARCHIVES

Infantry attacking the city center.

GERMAN FEDERAL ARCHIVES

A German Oberleutnant (1st Lieutenant) with a Soviet PPSh-41 machine gun.

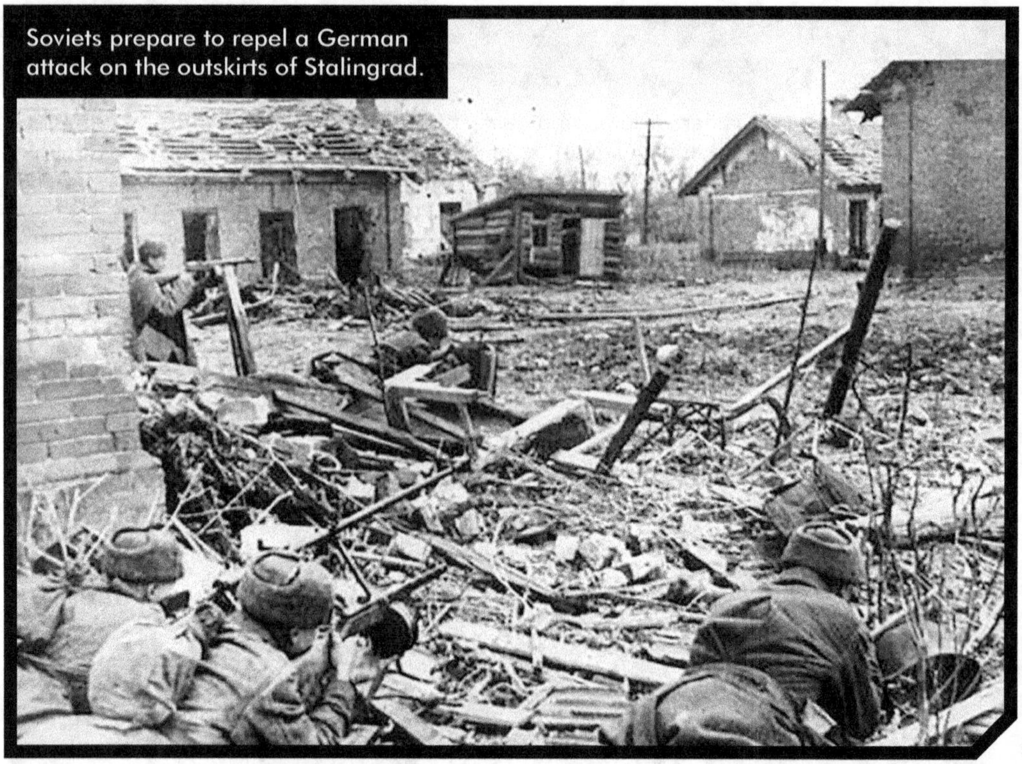

Soviets prepare to repel a German attack on the outskirts of Stalingrad.

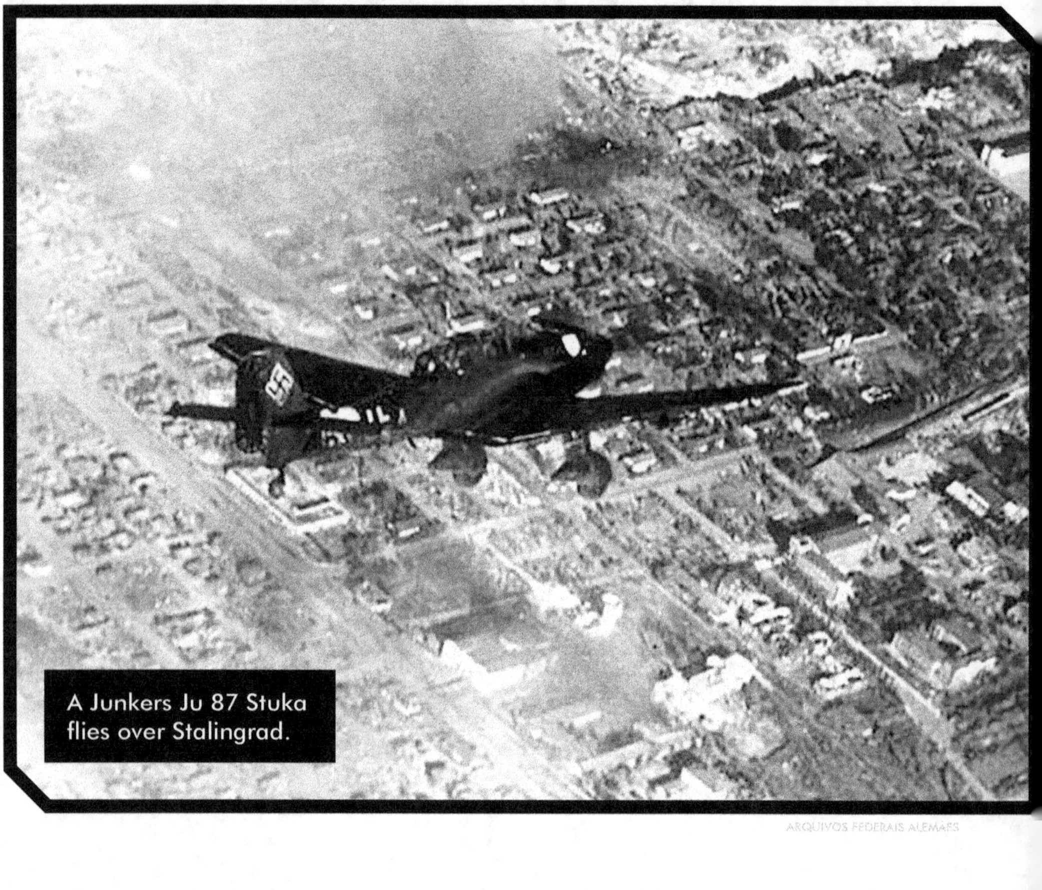

A Junkers Ju 87 Stuka flies over Stalingrad.

ARQUIVOS FEDERAIS ALEMÃES

Soviet soldiers attack a house (February 1943).

German soldiers taken as prisoners of war.

A Red Army
soldier takes a
German prisoner.

OPERATION TORCH

Between the 8th and 10th of November 1942, with the support of the Americans, the Allies launched Operation Torch, which aimed to combat forces from the Vichy Republic, who changed sides and began assisting the Allies, who surrounded the Axis forces in northern Tunisia and forced their surrender. In this way, Operation Torch fulfilled its objectives of ensuring victory in North Africa and introducing American armed forces into the fight against the Nazis. The operation opened a second battlefront that forced the German Army to move troops from the Soviet lines, giving the Soviets the opportunity to reorganize. The victory of the Allies in North Africa led to the Italian Campaign, which culminated in the fall of the fascist government in the country and the elimination of an important ally of the Germans.

US troops land near
Algiers, Algeria.

The USS Lakehurst (formerly Seatrain New Jersey) after unloading medium tanks at Safi, Morocco, for Operation Torch.

A shipment of Supermarine Spitfires in just 11 days by RAF, in Gibraltar, takes off for North Africa.

Hangar and Italian planes destroyed at Castel Benito airport in Tripoli.

American landing troops in North Africa.

British tanks in the port of Tripoli.

British and American troops on the coast near the city of Algiers.

Also called the Third and Fourth Battles of Savo Island, the Battle of Solomons, and the Battle of Friday the 13th, it was the scene of the deaths of two American Navy admirals, the only ones to be killed in an engagement during the war.

In early November 1942, the Japanese organized a transport convoy to take seven thousand soldiers to Guadalcanal, to try once again to retake the air base. In the battle, both sides lost several ships. Allied planes also sank most Japanese troop transports and prevented most troops and equipment from reaching Guadalcanal. The battle was a strategic victory for the US and the Allies.

Most of the battle took place in the area between Savo Island (center) and Guadalcanal (left).

An aerial view of Henderson Field on Guadalcanal in late August 1942.

Portland undergoing drydock repairs in Sydney, Australia, a month after the battle.

The USS Washington's cannons fire on Kirishima during the battle, November 15.

The Kinugawa Maru, one of four Japanese transports stranded and destroyed on Guadalcanal, November 15, 1942, photographed a year later.

Wreckage of the Japanese ship Maru Yamazuki on a beach on the island of Guadalcanal.

1943

The Warsaw Ghetto Uprising was an act of resistance in the Warsaw Ghetto, Poland. With the sending of 300,000 of the 380,000 people in the ghetto to the Treblinka extermination camp, where they were murdered immediately upon arrival, the rest of the ghetto's inhabitants knew what awaited them, and many preferred to die fighting. The uprising was crushed by the SS Gruppenführer Jürgen Stroop.

Jews being forcibly removed from their shelters in the Warsaw ghetto.

The Warsaw ghetto. This section of the street connected the "small" and the "big ghetto."

Jewish women of resistance, including Malka Zdrojewicz (right), who survived the Majdanek extermination camp.

The poster published by the Zionist resistance organization reads: "All people are equal; brown, white, black and yellow. Separating people, colors, races is yet another act of cheating!"

The leader of the major operation, SS Brigadeführer Jürgen Stroop.

Askaris or Trawnikis, snipers trained in concentration camps, examine the bodies of Jews killed in the repression of the revolt.

Captured Jews are taken by German troops to be deported.

An SS patrol on Nowolipie Street, inside the ghetto.

The destruction of a housing block.

Ghetto fires seen from the Żoliborz district.

A man jumps to his death from a window to avoid capture.

The Warsaw Ghetto area after the war.

ALLIED INVASION OF SICILY JULY 9 – AUGUST 17

Operation Husky, the Allied invasion of Sicily, was a successful campaign in which the Western powers seized this important island in the Mediterranean. It was the first stage of the invasion of Italy. The campaign featured a major naval operation and the deployment of paratroops, followed by six weeks of intense ground fighting. The deterioration of Italian armed resistance, among other reasons, led to the revolt of the Italians and the fall of their dictator, Benito Mussolini.

During the Allied invasion of Sicily, the Liberty ship Robert Rowan (K-40) explodes after being hit by a German Ju 88 bomber.

The Allied leaders of the campaign, General Eisenhower (first left) meets in North Africa with (foreground, left to right) Air Marshal Sir Arthur Tedder, General Sir Harold RLG Alexander, Admiral Sir Andrew B. Cunningham, and (top row) Mr. Harold Macmillan, Major General W. Bedell Smith, and unidentified British officers.

Erwin Rommel (left).

Troops of the British 51st Infantry Division unloading on the day of the Allied invasion of Sicily, July 10, 1943.

Invasion of Sicily. The occupants of the Eternity tank check out the vehicle after arriving at the Red Beach.

Wreckage of an Italian armored train, destroyed by the USS Bristol while seeking to prevent the landing at Licata.

Two British soldiers from the 6th Battalion, Durham Light Infantry, part of the British 50th Division, with an American paratrooper from the 505th Infantry Regiment, part of the US 82nd Airborne Division.

Italian prisoners of war.

The Canadians in Sicily: troops of the Loyal Edmonton Regiment, part of the 1st Canadian Division.

A Sherman tank overcomes the rough terrain of Sicily in mid-July 1943.

A wounded American soldier receiving blood plasma (August 9, 1943).

American soldiers observe a dead German pilot and his destroyed plane near Gela (July 12, 1943).

THE ALLIED INVASION OF ITALY

The Allied Invasion of Italy was a major landing on the Italian coast that took place on September 3, 1943, by soldiers of the 15th Army Group commanded by General Harold Alexander, which contained units of General Mark Clark's American 5th Army and General Bernard Montgomery's British 8th Army. The operation was carried out shortly after the successful invasion of Sicily during the Italian Campaign. The main forces landed in Salerno in the so-called Operation Avalanche, while additional forces landed in Calabria and Taranto. Fierce fighting ensued for 13 days, and despite intense and determined German counterattacks, the Allies gained their objectives and continued their invasion of the remainder of Mussolini's Italy.

Artillery being landed during the invasion of Italy at Salerno in September 1943.

Men of the 2nd Northamptonshire Regiment wait to embark in Sicily for the invasion of Italy on September 2, 1943.

Lieutenant General Mark Clark aboard USS Ancon during landing in Salerno, Italy, September 12, 1943.

The US Navy tank landing ship unloads an army jeep on an Italian beach. This photo may have been taken at one of the Salerno landings in September 1943.

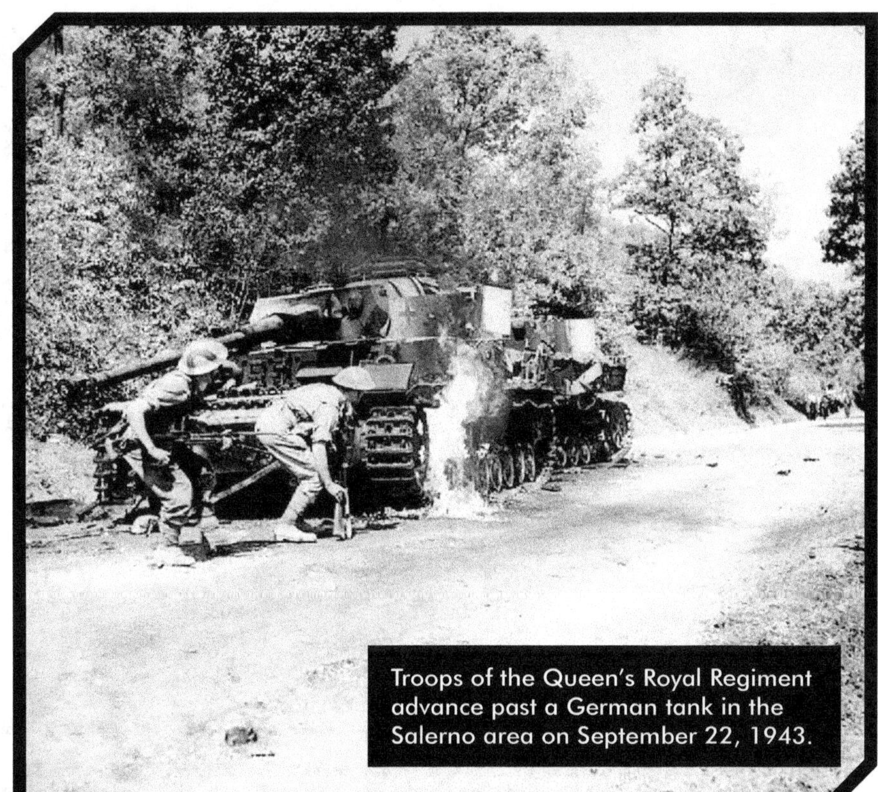

Troops of the Queen's Royal Regiment advance past a German tank in the Salerno area on September 22, 1943.

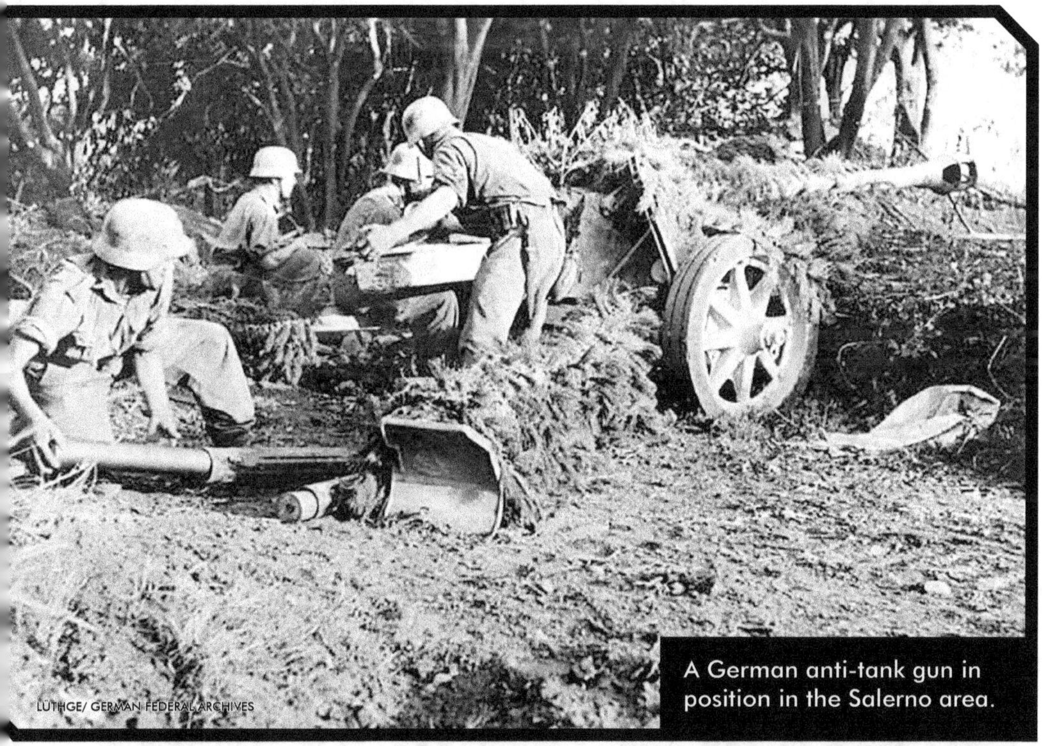

LÜTHGE/ GERMAN FEDERAL ARCHIVES

A German anti-tank gun in position in the Salerno area.

Albert Kesselring, Commander of German forces in Italy.

British troops enter the city of Salerno on September 10, 1943.

Ascending into Prato, Italy, men of the 370th Infantry Regiment must climb the mountain ahead, on April 9, 1945. 370th US Regiment advancing through Prato.

SECOND BATTLE OF SMOLENSK |AUGUST 7 – OCTOBER 8|

The Second Battle of Smolensk was a Soviet strategic offensive operation conducted by the Red Army, as part of the 1943 summer-autumn campaign. The battle of Smolensk was decisive, although it managed to advance only 155 miles. With the victory, the Soviet Union managed to push the Nazis away from Moscow, cutting a German front in half, which helped in the battle to cross the Dneiper, since the enemy troops were divided. With this achievement, the Soviets saw for the first time the war crimes and local destruction caused by the Nazis.

A Russian vehicle with smoke launchers, in August 1943.

SECOND BATTLE OF KYEV | NOVEMBER 3 – DECEMBER 22 |

The Second Battle of Kyev, also known as the Battle of the Dnieper, consisted of three strategic operations: two offensive and one defensive by the Red Army, as well as an operational counterattack by the Wehrmacht, which occurred shortly after the failed German offensive on Kursk.

A German panzer passes through Zhitomir, in November 1943.

Kyev is liberated by the Nazis. Soviet infantry marching down the main street, Kreschatik, in November 1943.

Soviet soldiers prepare rafts before crossing the Dnieper River in the Soviet Union in 1943 (the sign says "To Kyev!").

Soviet tanks during the Kyev offensive in November 1943.

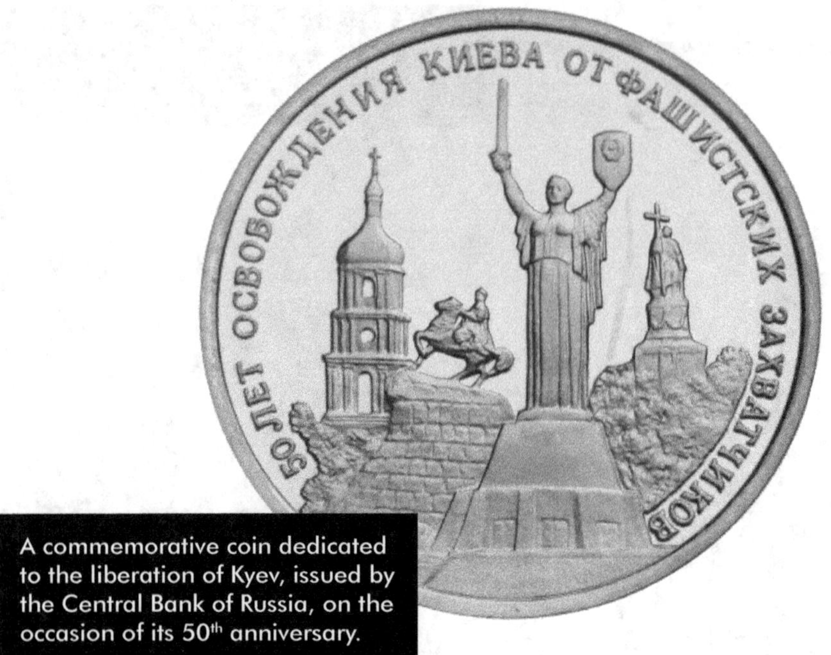

A commemorative coin dedicated to the liberation of Kyev, issued by the Central Bank of Russia, on the occasion of its 50th anniversary.

BATTLE OF TARAWA | NOVEMBER 20 – 23 |

The Battle of Tarawa took place during the Pacific War in November 1943. It was the United States' second major land offensive action of the war – following the Battle of Guadalcanal and the subsequent recapture of the Solomon Islands – and the first in the central Pacific Ocean.

Like all battles fought in the Pacific up to that point, the Americans faced strong Japanese resistance. The 4,500 Japanese entrenched on the atoll, well-armed and prepared, fought practically to the last man, causing more than 3,100 casualties to the Americans, the highest number of casualties – proportional to the total number of soldiers involved – of the entire war.

Marines attack Tarawa.

Training on the streets
of Hampton.

Marines seeking shelter among the dead
and wounded behind the sea wall of the
Red Beach, Tarawa.

The Colonel David Shoup command post at Red Beach.

A Marine sets fire to a Japanese casemate.

A flamethrower setting fire to an enemy fort in Tarawa.

North American LVTS and a Japanese Type 95 light tank, on Tarawa, after the battle.

Japanese prisoners of war.

Empty helmets and artillery shells used to mark the graves of Marines killed on Tarawa.

A long-range aircraft at Hawkins Field on Betio Island.

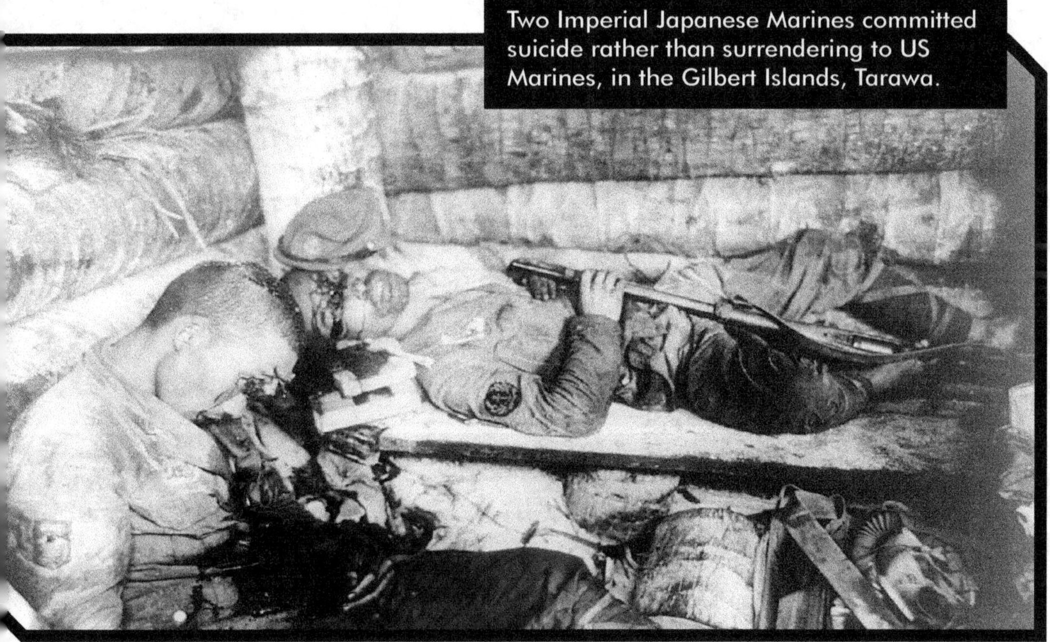

Two Imperial Japanese Marines committed suicide rather than surrendering to US Marines, in the Gilbert Islands, Tarawa.

BATTLE OF MAKIN

The Battle of Makin was fought between the United States Army and the Imperial Japanese Army forces as part of the War of the Pacific during World War II, on Makin Atoll in the Gilbert Islands. The complete occupation of Makin took four days and costed more lives for the Navy than for the personnel on the ground. Despite superiority in men and weapons, the 27th Division had several difficulties in subduing the island's defenders. One Japanese Ha-Go tank was destroyed in combat and the other two tanks were abandoned without having fired a shot.

Compared to the 395 Japanese killed in action, American troops on the ground suffered 218 casualties (66 killed and 152 wounded). The Navy's losses were much greater: 644 dead at Liscome Bay, 43 dead in a fire on the battleship USS Mississippi, and there were another 10 dead among landing personnel and airmen, totaling 697 deaths at sea for the US. Despite this, the total of 763 Americans killed does not even come close to the total losses suffered by the Japanese, who had their garrison on the island completely annihilated.

US troops fight on the coast of the Yellow Beach, on Butaritari Atoll, after a naval artillery bombardment.

A tank stuck in a crater opened by shells stops the soldiers' advance on the narrow causeway north of Lake Jill.

Two M3 tanks firing at Japanese positions.

American landing at Makin.

A Japanese shelter on Makin Atoll.

1944

BATTLE OF MONTE CASSINO | JANUARY 17 – MAY 19

The Battle of Monte Cassino, also known as the Battle of Rome, or the Battle of Cassino, was a series of four bitter battles fought by the Allies and the Axis to break the Winter Line and conquer Rome. After thousands of deaths and injuries and the destruction of one of the pillars of the Western Christian world, the Allies had Rome on the "horizon" and central Italy in their sights.

Royal Engineers from the British 46th Infantry Division cross the Garigliano River on January 19, 1944.

Even under grenade attacks, the German tank crew works hard to get the damaged tank back on the road.

ENZ/ GERMAN FEDERAL ARCHIVES

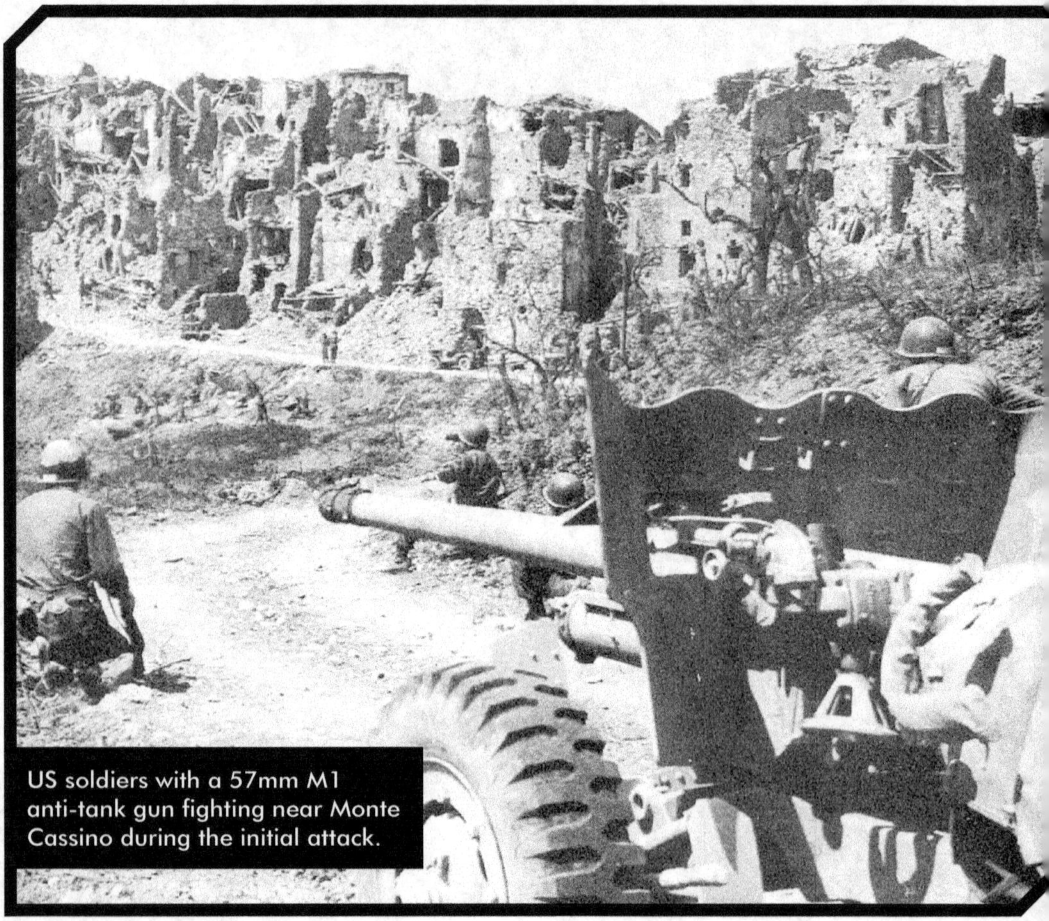

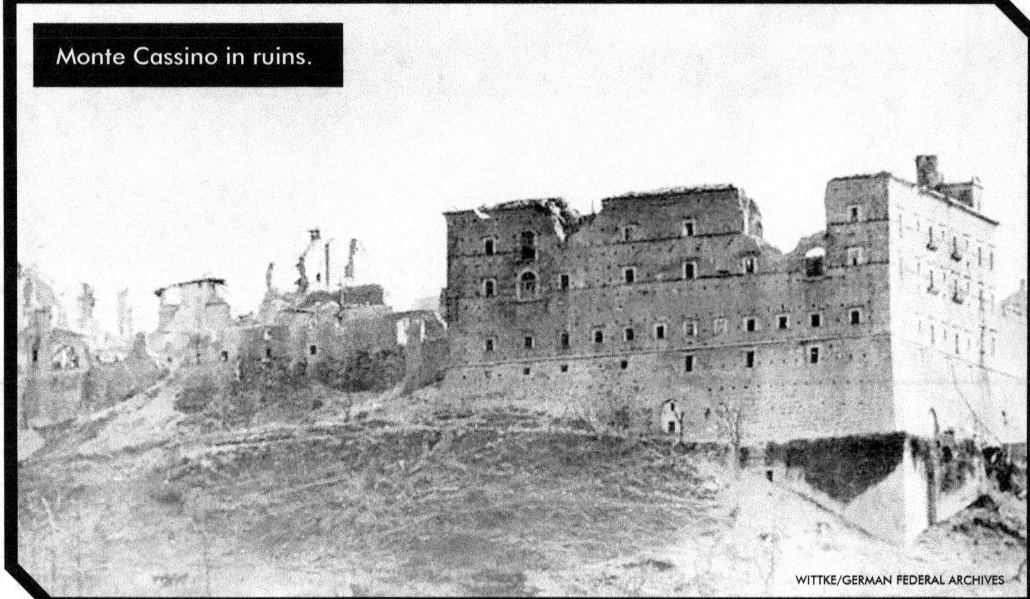

US soldiers with a 57mm M1 anti-tank gun fighting near Monte Cassino during the initial attack.

Monte Cassino in ruins.

WITTKE/GERMAN FEDERAL ARCHIVES

German prisoners captured by New Zealand troops.

GERMAN FEDERAL ARCHIVES

BATTLE OF MONTE CASTELLO

| JANUARY 17 – MAY 19 |

The Battle of Monte Castello was fought at the end of the Second World War, between Allied troops and the forces of the German Army, who were trying to contain their advance in Northern Italy. This battle marked the presence of the Brazilian Expeditionary Force (FEB) in the conflict. The battle dragged on for three months, from November 24, 1944, to February 21, 1945, during which six attacks were carried out, resulting in a large number of Brazilian casualties. Four of the attacks were unsuccessful due to strategic failures.

BRAZILIAN EXPEDITIONARY FORCE

Brazilian soldiers greet Italian civilians in the city of Massarosa, in September 1944.

DURVAL JR.

German General Otto Fretter-Pico, commander of the 148th Infantry Division, and Italian General Mario Carloni, on April 28, 1945.

1st GAVCA P-47 with the emblem "Senta a Pua!" ("Go for it!" or "Hit 'em hard!" in a loose translation), from the Brazilian Air Force.

Brazilian Fighter
Squadron emblem.

A company from the III Battalion of
the 11th Regiment of the Brazilian
Expeditionary Force in Italy.

BATTLE OF NORMANDY

Operation Overlord was the codename for the Battle of Normandy, an Allied operation that began the successful invasion of German-occupied Western Europe during World War II. The operation began on June 6, 1944, with the Normandy landings (Operation Neptune, also known as D-Day). An air attack by twelve hundred planes preceded an amphibious landing involving more than five thousand vessels. Around 160,000 men crossed the English Channel on June 6, and with that, more than three million Allies were in France by the end of August. The decision to carry out a cross-channel invasion in 1944 was made at the Trident Conference in Washington, D.C., in May 1943. General Dwight D. Eisenhower was appointed commander of the Supreme Headquarters, Allied Expeditionary Forces (SHAEF), and General Bernard Montgomery was appointed commander of the British 21st Army Group, which comprised all land forces involved in the invasion. The coast of Normandy was chosen as the site of the invasion, with the Americans assigned to land at Utah and Omaha Beaches, the British at Sword and Gold, and the Canadians at Juno. To meet the expected conditions, special technology was developed, including two artificial harbors called Mulberry Harbors and a series of specialized tanks nicknamed Hobart's Funnies. In the months leading up to the invasion, the Allies carried out a fake military operation, Operation Bodyguard, using electronic and visual disinformation. This false operation misled the Germans as to the date and location of the main Allied landing points. Adolf Hitler appointed Field Marshal Erwin Rommel responsible for developing fortifications along the Atlantic Wall in anticipation of an invasion.

The Allies failed to achieve their objectives on the first day but gained a tenuous position that was gradually expanded by capturing the port of Cherbourg on June 26, and the city of Caen on July 21. A counterattack by German forces failed on August 8, leading to 50,000 soldiers from the German 7th Army being captured in the Battle of the Falaise Pocket. The Allies began an invasion of southern France (Operation Dragoon) on 15 August 15, then the Liberation of Paris on August 25. German forces retreated across the Seine on August 30, 1944, marking the end of Operation Overlord.

Landing cargo ships coming ashore on Omaha Beach at low tide during the first days of the operation in mid-June 1944. Identifiable ships include: LST-532 (center of view); USS LST-262 (3rd LST from right); USS LST-310 (2nd LST from right); USS LST-533 (partially visible at far right); and USS LST-524.

Live ammunition
training exercise.

The British Army in the United Kingdom
during preparation for Operation Tonga,
part of the Normandy air invasion.

Soldiers of the "Free India" Legion wait at the
Atlantic Wall, in France, on March 21, 1944.

WETTE/ GERMAN FEDERAL ARCHIVES

Anti-tank steel obstacles on
the beach. Pas de Calais,
April 18, 1944.

JESSE/ GERMAN FEDERAL ARCHIVES

British pathfinders synchronize their watches in front of an Armstrong Whitworth Albemarle.

American soldiers, part of the US 1st Infantry Division, leaving a boat in Omaha.

THE HOLOCAUST

The term "Holocaust," which in Greek means a sacrificial offering, designates, in its capitalized form, the attempted extermination of groups considered unwanted by the Nazis during the Third Reich. The victims were mainly Jews, but also communists, homosexuals, gypsies, physically and mentally disabled people, Soviet prisoners of war, members of the Polish, Soviet, and other Slavic intellectual elite, political activists, Jehovah's Witnesses, some Catholic and Protestant priests, unionists, psychiatric patients and common criminals. They all perished side by side in concentration and extermination camps.

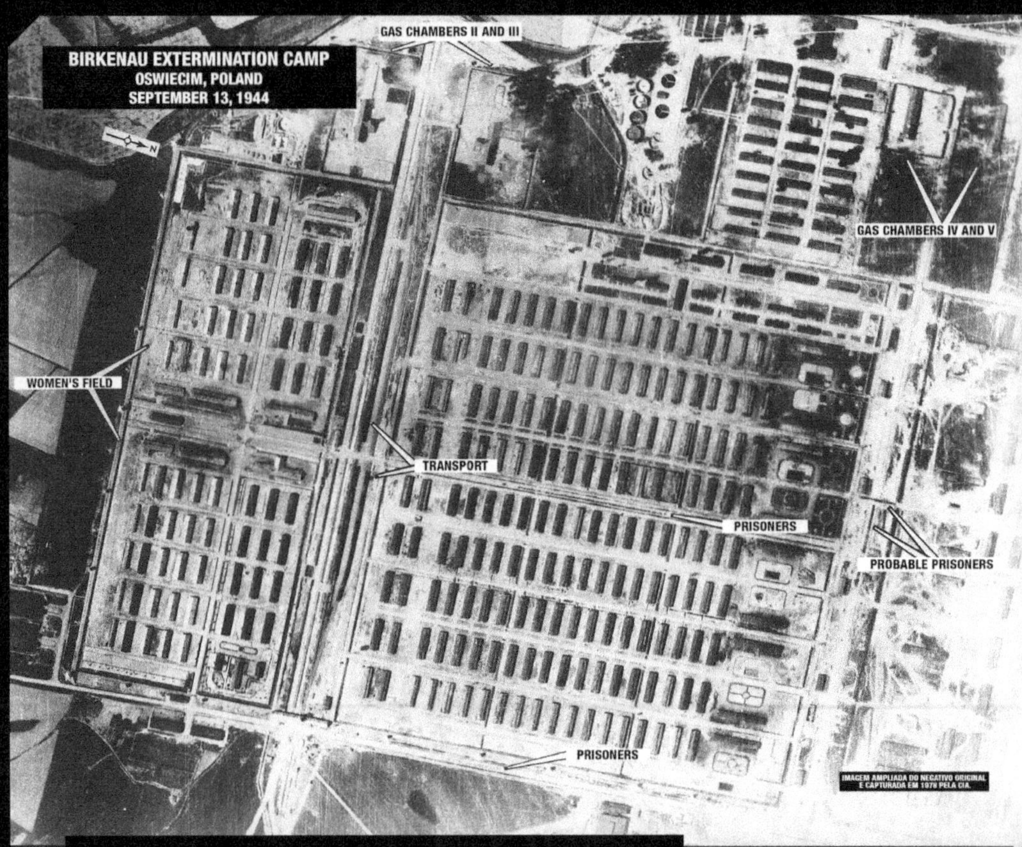

The Auschwitz-Birkenau concentration camp, where more than a million people were murdered.

Mass grave of Jews in Zolochiv, Ukraine.

The bodies of prisoners executed at the Buchenwald extermination camp.

A prison ID of a 14-year-old Polish girl sent to the Auschwitz camp for forced labor in December 1942.

SS soldiers next to the bodies of Jews who committed suicide so as not to be captured alive (Warsaw Ghetto, 1943).

Bodies of prisoners piled up on the outskirts of the Belsen camp (c. 1945).

Thousands of gold rings taken from Holocaust victims.

Corpses of prisoners from
Mauthausen-Gusen (May 1945).

BATTLE OF SAIPAN

The Battle of Saipan was one that formed part of a series of conflicts in the Marianas region during the War of the Pacific. It began on June 15 with the landing of American troops on the island of Saipan after intense naval bombardment. Until then, the island was occupied by the Japanese Army under the command of General Yoshitsugu Saito.

After the Allied victory, the island became a North American aviation base of great importance for the operations that followed in the Mariana Islands and for the invasion of the Philippines in October of that same year, as well as a base for bombers that attacked Japanese cities in the final months of the war.

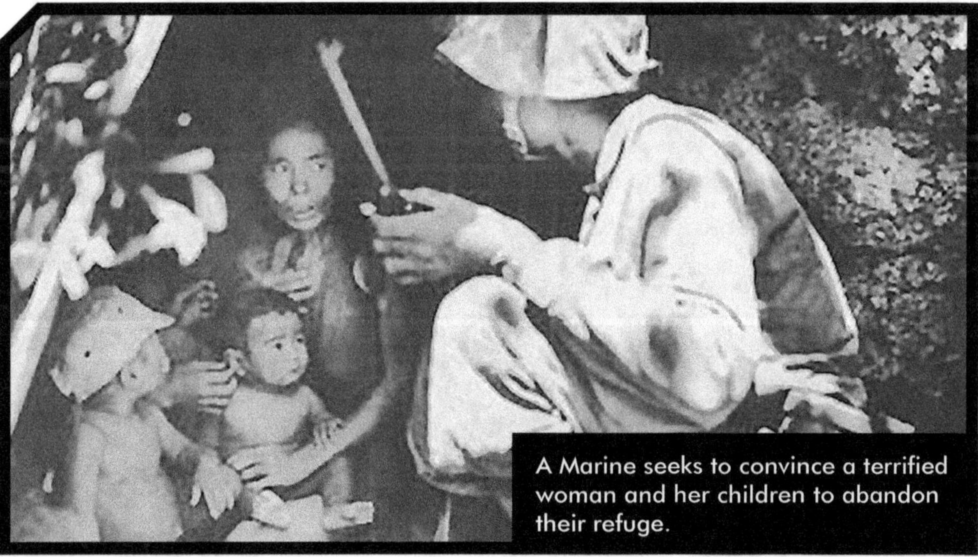

Marines take cover behind one of their tanks as they advance toward the northern tip of Saipan Island, July 8, 1944.

Carrying a Colt M1911, a Marine moves cautiously through the jungle of Saipan, July 1944.

BATTLE OF GUAM

The Second Battle of Guam was a conflict between the Americans and the Japanese in an attempt to retake the island of Guam, a US territory in the Mariana Islands captured by the Japanese in 1941, in the First Battle of Guam at the beginning of the Pacific War.

The first flag on Guam.

Bombing of Guam on July 14, 1944 before the battle.

An infantry regiment soldier killed after an attack on Gyokusai, Guam, July 29.

Three amphibian battalion officers who played a major role in the invasion of Guam (from left to right): Maj Erwin F. Wann, Maj W. W. Butler, and Lt. Col. Sylvester Stephens.

US Marines show their appreciation for the Coast Guard. It reads: "Marines salute Coast Guard for their big part in the invasion of Guam. They put us here and we intend to stay."

The Battle of Tinian was one of the conflicts of the Pacific War, fought on the island of Tinian in the Mariana Islands as part of the Allied offensive to retake the islands in the region. The Japanese garrison of approximately nine thousand soldiers was eliminated, and the island joined Saipan and Guam as a base for the United States Air Force.

Marines land on Tinian.

Marines who were patrolling the island of Tinian move into firing position when they are spotted by the enemy.

Marines check a Japanese tank.

A Japanese plane destroyed on Tinian Island, July 30, 1944.

Japanese soldiers killed in a suicide attack on the night of July 23rd to 24th.

US Marine and a child at the barbed wire fence of the Tinian detention.

It was the code name for the so-called Belarusian Offensive, which took place between June 22 and August 19, 1944. The name was given in honor of Prince Pyotr Bagration, then a general of Soviet forces injured in the Battle of Borodino during the Napoleonic Wars. The action resulted in the almost complete destruction of the Army Group Center and three of its components: the 4th Army, the 9th Army, and the 9th Panzer Army.

The Soviet military triumph was due to the coordinated movement of the offensive on all fronts and operations to deceive the enemy until the general offensive in the summer of 1944. Despite the large number of forces involved in the operation, the enemy had no idea when or where the attack would take place.

After the battle, the German army had lost around 25% of all forces on the Eastern Front, never recovering from the huge loss.

Nazi officer losses: nine generals were killed, 22 captured, one lost, and two who committed suicide. At the end of the operation, the Army Group Center was almost completely destroyed.

Material losses: 2,000 tanks and 57,000 vehicles, as well as around 400,000 deaths. Losses on the Soviet side: 2,957 tanks, 2,447 artillery pieces, and 822 aircraft. Human losses: 180,040 dead and missing, and 590,848 wounded.

Over the two months of the battle, the Red Army suffered 25% of the Wehrmacht's losses, liberating countless cities. To demonstrate victory to other countries, around 50,000 German prisoners of war captured east of Minsk marched for around 90 minutes through the streets of Moscow, after which the streets were deliberately washed with soap and water. The confrontation resulted in the biggest defeat for Germany's army in World War II.

A German soldier in a tank at an observation post.

WILTBERGER MEYER/GERMAN FEDERAL ARCHIVES

Two German tanks belonging to the 20th Panzer Division destroyed in June 1944.

Civilians carry belongings taken from burning houses in July 1944.

The Warsaw Uprising was an armed struggle in which the Armia Krajowa (Polish Underground Army) attempted to liberate the city from Nazi control. The action began on August 1, 1944, at 5 p.m., as part of a national act that was supposed to last a few days, just enough for the Red Army to reach Warsaw, but the advance was stopped by German forces, which delayed the reinforcement of the Poles. The revolt, however, lasted for 63 days, until, on October 2, the Poles surrendered to the Germans.

The offensive began as the Soviets approached the capital. The Polish Army intended to keep the Germans occupied, give the Soviets time to reach the city, and aid in the war efforts against the Axis forces. Among the secondary objectives was the liberation of Warsaw before the arrival of the Soviet Union, in order to gain its right to sovereignty and undo the division of Western Europe into spheres of influence under the Allied powers. The hope was to be able to reinstate their country's authorities before the Polish-Soviet National Liberation Committee took control. At first, the Poles isolated substantial areas of the capital, but the Red Army did not approach the region until mid-September. Inside the city, an intense conflict between Poles and Germans ensued. On September 16, the Soviets captured territory within meters of Polish positions on the banks of the Vistula River but made no advances during the rest of the uprising. This chapter led to accusations that Stalin hoped for the revolt to fail so that he could unquestionably occupy Poland. Currently, this is the version most confirmed by Polish history, as Stalin had allied with Germany in the invasion and division of Polish territories in 1939 and was also responsible for the massacres of countless citizens, especially the Katyn Massacre, where more than 20,000 Polish army officers and civilians were murdered in the Katyn Forest, Russia, on direct orders from Moscow. During the entire period of Soviet occupation in the country, between 1945 and 1989, it could mean a risk of imprisonment and even death to insinuate that the Soviet government was involved in the massacre, as the government's official version was that what happened was just another of the crimes committed by the Nazis during the war.

Although the exact numbers remain unknown, it is estimated that 16,000 members of the Polish resistance were killed and 6,000 were seriously injured. Between 150,000 and 200,000 civilians died, most of them victims of massacres carried out by Axis troops. German casualties were approximately 16,000 soldiers killed and nine thousand wounded. During the fighting, an estimated 25% of Warsaw's buildings were destroyed. Shortly after the Polish surrender, Nazi troops systematically destroyed block by block, around 35% of the city. Adding up all the damage suffered by the capital since the invasion in 1939, more than 85% of the city was destroyed when the Soviet Army finally crossed its borders.

German soldiers fighting the Polish resistance on Theater Square in Warsaw in September 1944.

SEIDEL/GERMAN FEDERAL ARCHIVES

Members of the Russian Liberation Army during the Warsaw Uprising in August 1944.

Waffen-SS members in local combat. Warsaw, August 1944.

OPERATION DRAGON

Also known as the D-Day Landing, it was a decisive step in the liberation of France from Nazism. On August 15, 1944, allied troops disembarked in the Provence region, the majority of whom were made up of Africans from the then colonies, who suffered heavy casualties with the German invasion, which took place in 1940. The attack was considered a success by Allied forces, as with more ports, the Allies were able to get more supplies to fight the Axis in Europe.

The combatant and politician André Diethelm reviews the troops liberated in August 1944, in Marseille.

BATTLE OF ARNHEM | SEPTEMBER 17 – 26 |

The conflict that involved the forces of the German Army and the Allies took place in the Dutch cities of Arnhem, Wolfheze, Oosterbeek, and Driel, also reaching the interior of the country. The conquest of France and Belgium in the summer of 1944 excited Allied troops in an attempt to invade the Netherlands, so Field Marshal Bernard Montgomery's decision was to organize the advance towards the lower Rhine River, enabling the British 2nd Army to overcome the Siegfried line, one of the German defenses, and launch an attack on the Ruhr region.

To open a faster path to the industrial heart of the Third Reich, the so-called Operation Market Garden was launched on September 17th, the largest operation involving the launch of paratroopers in history. The idea was to conquer important bridges and cities and thus allow friendly troops to advance. The control of the bridges went as planned, and the Allies managed to liberate the cities of Eindhoven and Nijmegen. It was necessary to reach the Arnhem City Bridge, the furthest of all. However, the Germans were faster. Supplies and ammunition in the aircraft were scarce, and problems with radio equipment made it impossible to coordinate the attack with tanks on the ground. After a few days, a small British fighting force at Arnhem Bridge was attacked by the German Division, becoming trapped in a pocket near the river. There were nine days of intense combat until the British paratroopers ended up retreating in an action called "Operation Berlin." The conflict resulted in heavy casualties for the British parachute division (around 75%), and they have not participated in further combat since.

Walter Model and Heinz Harmel in a meeting during the Battle of Arnheim.

PETER ADENDORF/GERMAN FEDERAL ARCHIVES

British paratroopers in German captivity, September 1944.

ERICH WENZEL/ GERMAN FEDERAL ARCHIVES

British troops maintain brigade headquarters. September 1944.

BATTLE OF PELELIU | SEPTEMBER 15 – NOVEMBER 27 |

Fought between the Americans and the Japanese, the battle took place on the small island of Peleliu, belonging to the Republic of Palau. Originally made up of the 1st Marine Division, the American forces, commanded by Major General William Rupertus, had the support of Army troops from the 81st Infantry Division in a fight whose objective was to capture an airstrip located on a coral island. The North American fighters were counting on victory; however, they were surprised by the well-structured Japanese fortifications, in addition to the brutal resistance, causing the confrontation to last for around two months. The fighting resulted in the deaths of 28,000 Marines and other infantry troops. Considering all the battles that took place during the Pacific War, it was the one with the highest average number of victims.

A wounded marine receives hydration.

The exposed skull signals danger in the combat area. October 1944.

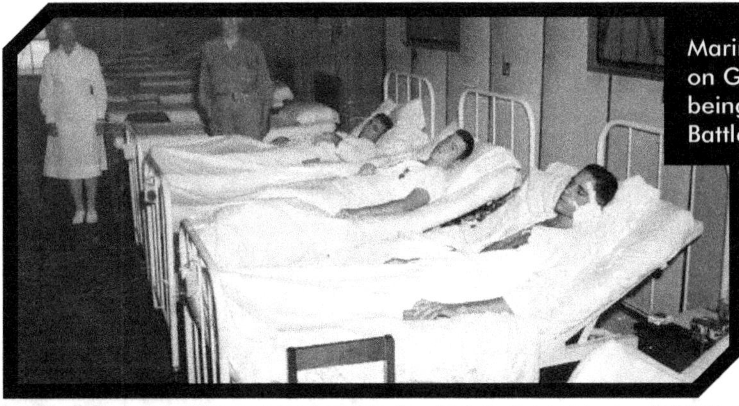

Marines in a hospital on Guadalcanal after being wounded in the Battle of Peleliu.

BATTLE OF AACHEN | OCTOBER 2 – 21 |

The Battle of Aachen was a conflict that took place in the city of the same name, on the border between Germany, the Netherlands, and Belgium. In September 1944, the Wehrmacht retreated to the German border after the defeat in France by the Allies. During the battle in France, German commanders estimated the size of their forces at 25 full divisions; in the same period, the German Army operated with 74 divisions in French territory. Even with heavy losses, the Germans managed to retreat to the Siegfried line and rebuild part of their forces, increasing the number of soldiers in the region to 230,000 by the end of the year. Despite little training and scarce weapons, this troop had good defensive positions and fortifications on the Siegfried line. In September, the first fighting reached the outskirts of Aachen and the German commander of the city offered to surrender to the North American Army. However, his letter of surrender was discovered by the SS during a raid on the city amid the evacuation of civilians. Hitler then ordered the commander's arrest and replaced him and his men with fighters from the 246th Volksgrenadier Division under the command of Gerhard Wilck. As a result, the Americans would have no choice but to conquer the territory by force.

The city was surrounded by the 1st and 30th Infantry Divisions, with the support of other units, and the plan was to take it by attacking from all sides. The territory was defended by the LXXXI Army Corps, which included four infantry divisions and two weakened tank formations. During the conflict, the Germans received approximately 24 thousand men as reinforcements, and also some troops from the 1st SS Division Leibstandarte Adolf Hitler. Despite being inferior in numbers, the defense had several casemates and fortifications on the outskirts of the city. The 30th Infantry Division's offensive began on October 2 and was immediately repulsed by the German defense. Bombing by planes and heavy ground artillery failed to force the Germans to retreat, but neither did it reduce the morale of the troops, and as a result, the Allied attacks north of the city were also unsuccessful.

The American 1st Infantry Division launched its offensive on October 8 and captured some of its objectives in the first 48 hours, despite suffering several setbacks due to constant German counterattacks. Meanwhile, the 30th Infantry Division continued to advance slowly, although, on October 12, they were still unable to link up with the 1st Division and complete the siege around the city. With that, the 1st Division dispatched the 26th Infantry Regiment and prepared for a direct attack on the city before the troops could assemble. Fighting within the city began on October 13th and dragged on until the 21st, with heavy casualties on both sides. Despite relentless German resistance, General Wilck decided to surrender and hand Aachen over to the Allies on October 21, ending the battle. During the entire conflict, the American Army suffered at least five thousand casualties, including dead, wounded, and missing, while the Germans lost more than five thousand soldiers, and around 5,600 men were taken as prisoners.

German soldiers advance through a clearing in the forest around Aachen, Germany.

GERMAN FEDERAL ARCHIVES

German infantry soldiers in a combat vehicle.

WAHNER/GERMAN FEDERAL ARCHIVES

A German gunner loading an anti-aircraft cannon.

German prisoners captured with the fall of Aachen, marching into captivity through the city's ruined streets.

BATTLE OF HÜRTGEN FOREST
| SEPTEMBER 19, 1944 – FEBRUARY 10, 1945 |

The battle, which involved several bloody clashes between the American and German forces, took place in the forest of Hürtgen. At first, the US intended to take Schmidt, liberate Monschau, and detain the German forces in the area, in order to prevent the reinforcement of the northern front lines in the Battle of Aachen, where German and American troops fought in the so-called Siegfried line. The second stage would be to advance towards the Rur River. The fastest route was through the Hürtgen Forest, but the decision to advance into the dense forest was a fatal error. The rugged soil of the region, as well as the incessant rain and fog, followed by snow and low temperatures ended up disorienting the Americans, turning the place into a stage for true carnage. The American soldiers who fought in the forest nicknamed the place the "Death Factory." The battle at Hürtgen left the 1st American Army with a balance of 33 thousand men, including dead and wounded. The casualties suffered by the Germans reached 28 thousand. Starting in September 1944 until February 1945, the conflict was considered the longest ever fought on German soil during the entire Second World War, in addition to being the longest ever fought by the North American Army.

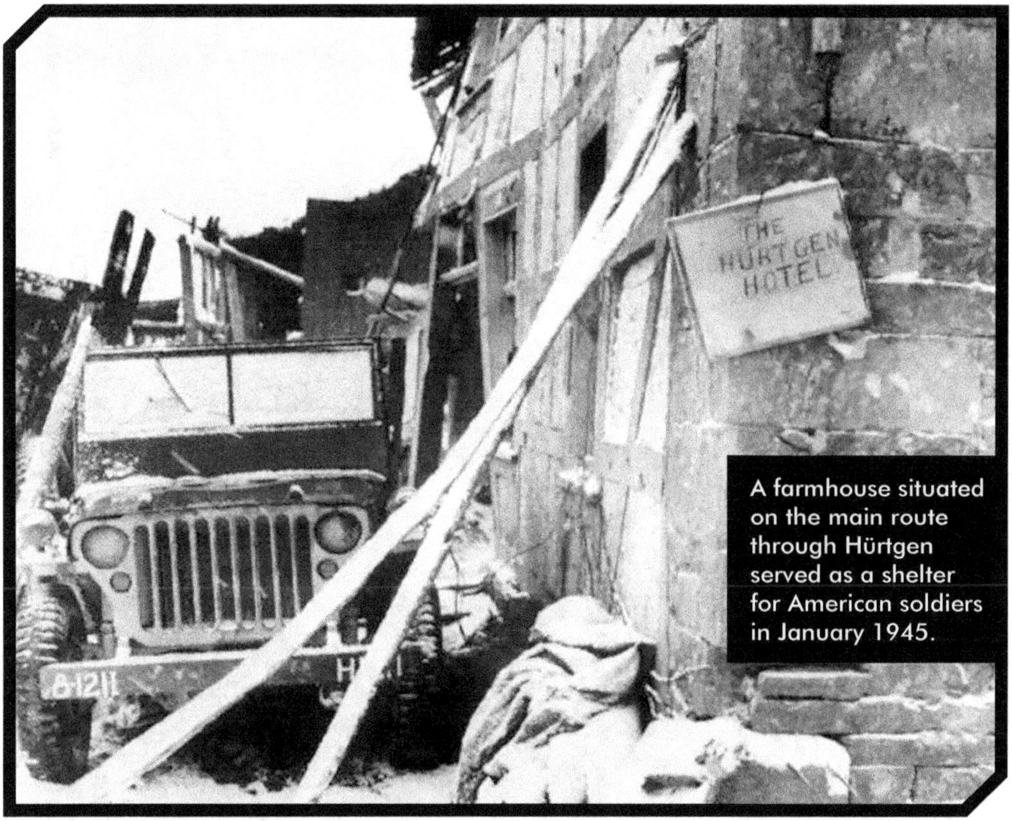

A farmhouse situated on the main route through Hürtgen served as a shelter for American soldiers in January 1945.

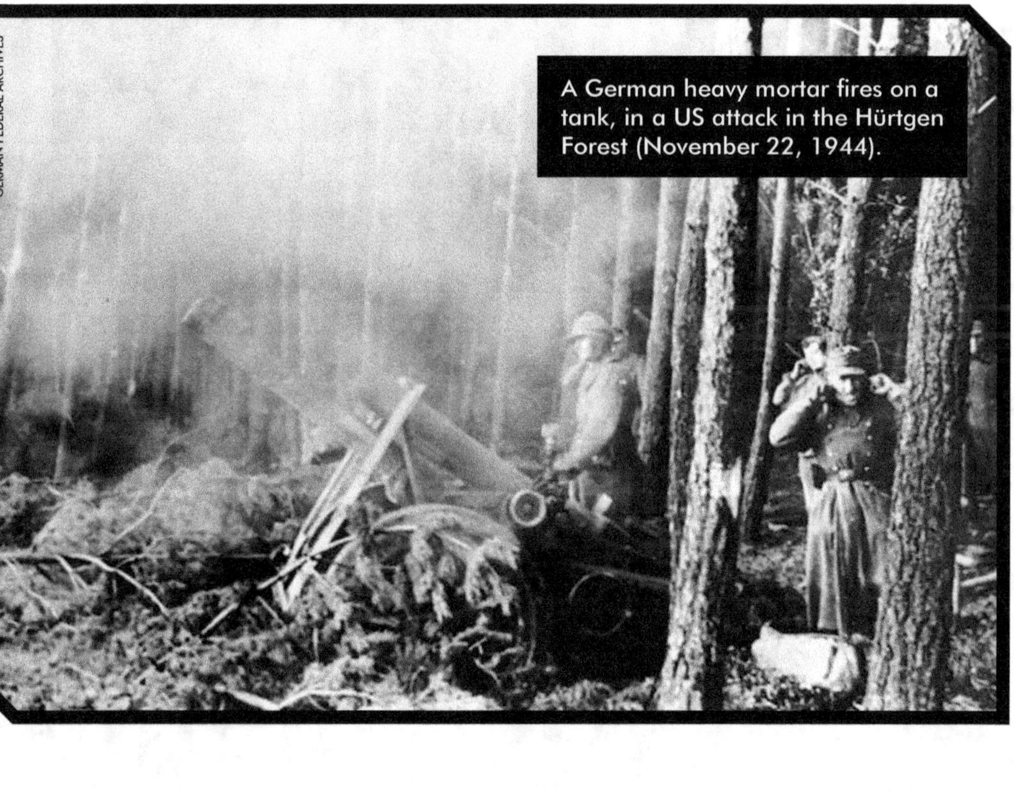

GERMAN FEDERAL ARCHIVES

A German heavy mortar fires on a tank, in a US attack in the Hürtgen Forest (November 22, 1944).

BATTLE OF LEYTE GULF | OCTOBER 23 – 26 |

The largest naval battle of World War II took place in the waters off one of the Philippine islands called Leyte Island. The combat took place during the Pacific War between Japan and Allied forces, who invaded the place to eliminate supply lines between the Japanese and the colonies in Southeast Asia, in particular, the supply of fuel to the Imperial Japanese Navy.

In an effort to stop the landing of Allied troops, Japanese soldiers gathered all their naval troops, however, the operation failed, resulting in many casualties.

With its naval force highly compromised, it became impossible for the Imperial Japanese Navy to engage in combat again, so it had to wait for the end of the war anchored in its own territory. It was on the island of Leyte that the first Japanese kamikazes launched themselves against the North American fleet in the Pacific Theater of Operations.

An American aircraft carrier in flames shortly after being hit by a Japanese bomb during an operation in the Philippines, October 24, 1944.

Salute from the crew of the Japanese aircraft carrier Zuikaku when the flag was lowered during the Battle of Cape Engaño, in October 1944.

Operation Queen was an Anglo-American action directed against the River Rur, on the Western Front of the German Siegfried line, as a stopping point for a further push along the river to the Rhine in Germany.

The offensive began on November 16, 1944, with one of the most intense Allied bombing raids of the war. However, the advance of Allied troops against German resistance was surprisingly slow, especially in the Hürtgen Forest, where the main advance of the offensive took place. In December, the Allies finally managed to reach the River Rur and tried to capture the most important dams, when the German Army launched its offensive called "Wacht am Rhein." The ensuing Battle of the Ardennes led to the immediate end of the Allied offensive efforts in Germany until February 1945.

(Left to right) Bradley, Gerow, Eisenhower, and Collins.

Rundstedt (middle) and Model (left) while planning the Ardennes Offensive.

Captured Tiger II with improvised American emblems.

BATTLE OF THE BULGE
| DECEMBER 16, 1944 – JANUARY 25, 1945 |

Also known as the Ardennes Offensive, it was the great German counter-offensive on the Western Front, launched at the end of the Second World War in the Ardennes Forest, located in the Wallonia region, Belgium, also reaching France and Luxembourg. The German Army called the action "Operation Vigil on the Rhine." This German offensive was officially called the Ardennes-Alsace Campaign by the US Army, although it became known as the Battle of the Ardennes Pocket, or "Bulge."

The offensive was supported by several small operations, such as Unternehmen Bodenplatte, Greif, and Währung. The Germans' goal was to divide the American and British Allies by capturing the region of Antwerp, Belgium, surrounding and destroying the Allied troops, and forcing them to negotiate a peace treaty with the Axis powers. With these objectives achieved, Hitler could focus his entire army against the Soviets on the Eastern Front.

The operation was planned in secret, with little information via radio, and with troop movements always taking place at night, with the aim of deceiving the Allied intelligence, which was unable to anticipate the operation, imagining that a large movement of soldiers would be obvious to reconnaissance aircraft.

The Allied forces were completely caught by surprise and their defense lines were dispersed, in addition to facing a very resistant enemy. Intense conflicts occurred in mild weather, especially near the city of Bastogne, and the terrain that favored the Allies delayed the enemy troops. American reinforcements, including American General George Patton's potent 3rd Army, as well as increasingly better weather conditions and great air superiority, allowed the German Army and its supply lines to be decimated, especially by the Allied Air Force, which ensured the failure of the operation.

US Army paratroopers are dropped
near Grave (Netherlands) at the start of
Operation Market Garden.

Belgian civilians killed
by German units
during the offensive.

Columns of captured American soldiers.

GERMAN FEDERAL ARCHIVES

German field commanders plan the advance.

COURTESY GERMAN FEDERAL ARCHIVES

1945

The Prague Offensive was the Soviet Union's last major operation on the European stage of World War II. The battle lasted from May 6 to 11, 1945, alongside the Prague uprising. All soldiers of the German Army Group Center were captured or killed.

Marshal Konev saluting the Soviets as they enter Prague, May 9, 1945.

Olshansky, Prague cemetery: an honorable burial place of Soviet soldiers who died during the liberation of the city.

OPERATION SPRING AWAKENING

This major German military offensive took place on the Eastern Front in Hungary, between March 6 and 16, 1945. It began with a secret and carefully elaborated strategy by the German Army in the Lake Balaton region, where its last fuel reserves were located. For this attack, the units that remained from the Ardennes Offensive, in which they were defeated, were used.

The surprise attack was successful, but the German Army did not count on the heavy counteroffensive launched by the Soviets, which ended up forcing its withdrawal. It didn't take long for the Russians to advance towards Berlin and Hungary.

German casualties.

WILFRIED WOSCIDLO/ GERMAN FEDERAL ARCHIVES

German Tiger II tanks armed with a long gun, ready to go into action.

HAMANN/ GERMAN FEDERAL ARCHIVES

BATTLE OF MANILA

The Battle of Manila was the largest urban combat of the Pacific War, which took place between the Americans, Filipinos, and Japanese for possession of the capital of the Philippines, during a counterattack by the Allies in the Southeast Asian theater of war. The battle was bloody and destroyed the entire city, resulting in Japanese rule in the Philippines for three years.

The city of Manila destroyed after the battle that bore its name in May 1945.

Manila is declared an "open city."

Manila citizens run from the Japanese-burned suburbs in search of safety.

US troops at the Rizal baseball stadium, Manila, on February 16, 1945.

Fire damage to the Manila Post Office in 1945.

BATTLE OF IWO JIMA | FEBRUARY 19 – MARCH 26 |

The Battle of Iwo Jima, or Operation Detachment, was fought between the United States and Japan, between February and March 1945, during the Pacific War. As a result, the Americans gained control of the island of Iwo Jima and the airfields on that same island. The fighting was vigorous, especially due to Japanese preparation, but American troops captured the island's highest point, Mount Suribachi. At the end of the confrontation, almost seven thousand American men lost their lives, compared to 21 thousand Japanese. The reason for the invasion of Iwo Jima was to capture its airfields, to provide a landing and refueling site for American bombers advancing toward Japan, while also making it possible for fighter escort of the bombers.

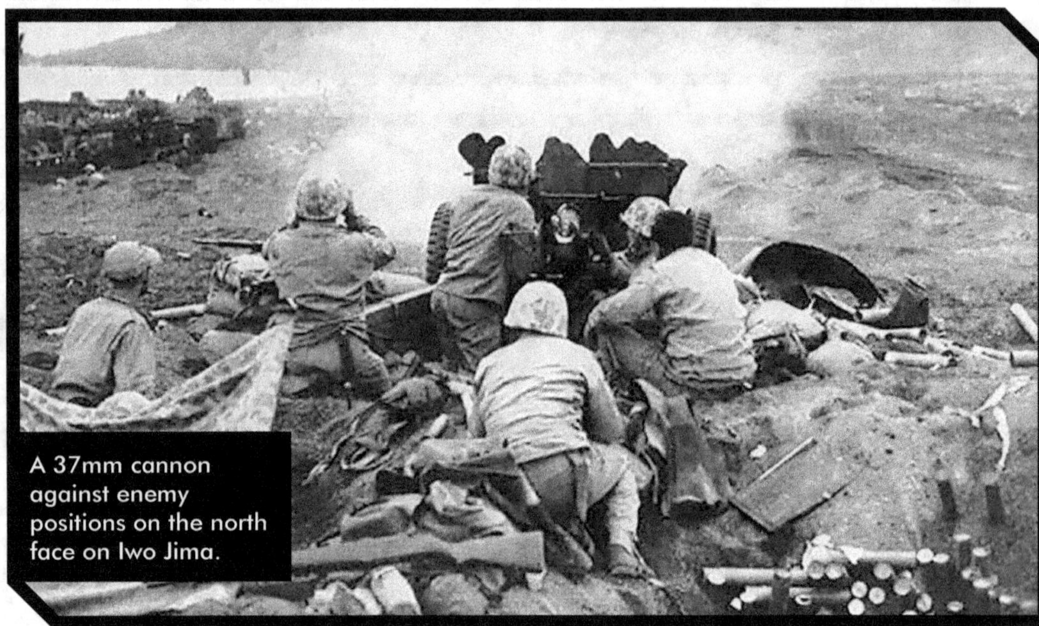

A 37mm cannon against enemy positions on the north face on Iwo Jima.

An American warship shelling Japanese defenses on Iwo Jima.

Marines landing
on the beach.

A flamethrower tank burns
important Japanese positions.

Lieutenant Wade discusses the global importance of the target in a pre-invasion briefing.

BATTLE OF HALBE | APRIL 24 – MAY 1 |

The Battle of Halbe was a confrontation between the German Army and the Red Army. The 9th German Army, then commanded by Colonel-General Theodor Busse, was practically annihilated in a battle for the occupation of Berlin.

The 12th Army, led by General Walther Wenck, was trying to advance west with the intention of surrendering to the Western Allies. To do this, they sought to break the siege formed by Soviet troops, commanded by Ivan Konev, at the same time that Marshal Georgy Zhukov's soldiers were fighting German soldiers to the northwest. The 9th Army sought to link up with the Western Allies passing through a village in Halbe, but ended up trapped in a pocket in the forest on the banks of the River Spree. Only a third of the German army achieved the objective, with the remainder captured by the Soviets. The confrontation resulted in the loss of 30,000 German soldiers.

Field Marshal Günther von Kluge (left) with Colonel General Gotthard Heinrici analyzing maps.

BATTLE OF BERLIN | APRIL 16 – MAY 2 |

The result of the Soviet offensive against German forces, the Battle of Berlin was the last in the European theater of war. Its strategy called for the simultaneous launch of several attacks in eastern Europe, from the Baltic Sea to the Carpathian region, with the aim of invading the countries still occupied by the Germans, reaching Berlin, and ending the war before the Allies on the Western Front entered the capital of the Reich. At the end of this confrontation, Adolf Hitler committed suicide and, a few days later, Germany surrendered.

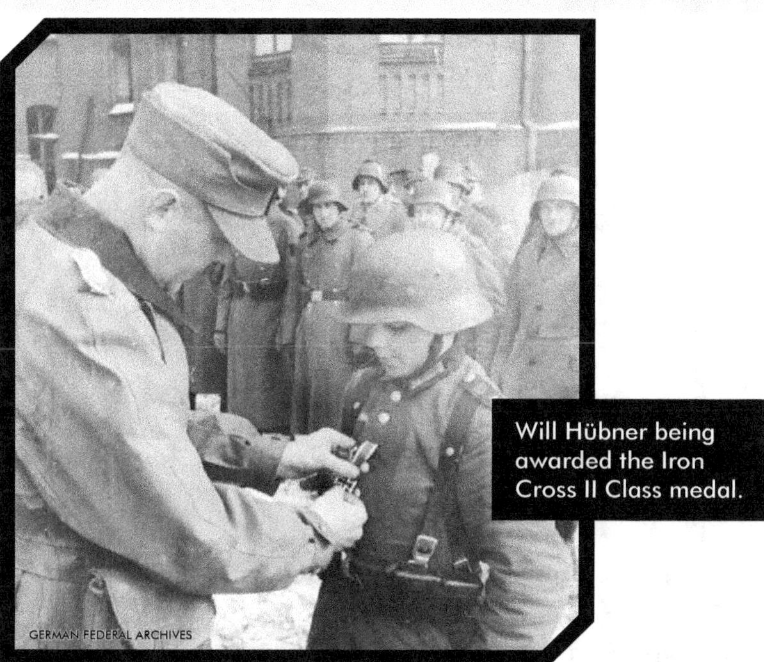

Will Hübner being awarded the Iron Cross II Class medal.

2nd Lieutenant William Robertson and Lieutenant Alexandre Sylvashko in front of the "East Meets West" poster, symbolizing the historic meeting of the Soviet and American Armies.

German women washing clothes at a cold-water hydrant on a Berlin street. A German armored vehicle is next to them (July 3, 1945).

German soldiers in Berlin. March 1945.

Field Marshal Wilhelm Keitel signs the act of unconditional surrender of the German Army on May 8, 1945.

BATTLE OF OKINAWA | APRIL 1 – JUNE 22 |

Taking place on the island of the same name, in the Ryukyu archipelago, in the south of Japan's four largest islands, it was the largest sea-land-air battle in history. Neither side had any idea that it would be the last major battle of World War II. The Americans planned Operation Downfall, the invasion of Japan's main islands, which never happened because of the Japanese surrender in August 1945, which took place after the use of atomic bombs on Hiroshima and Nagasaki.

The inhabitants of Okinawa called this battle "Tetsu no ame," and "Tetsu no bōfū," which mean, respectively, "rain of iron" and "violent wind of steel," referring to the intensity of fire during the combat.

In some battles like Iwo Jima, there were no civilians, but there was a large population in Okinawa. Civilian casualties counted at least 130,000 people, while US casualties reached 72,000, of which 15,900 killed or missing, twice as many as on Iwo Jima and Guadalcanal combined.

Child soldiers
captured in the
Battle of Okinawa.

American aircraft carrier
USS Bunker Hill in
flames after being hit by
two kamikaze planes.

US Marines walk past a
dead Japanese soldier in a
destroyed village, April 1945.

A Japanese
prisoner of war
sits behind barbed
wire after he and
306 others were
captured in the last
24 hours of the
battle by the 6th
Marine Division.

A group of Japanese prisoners captured on the island of Okuku in June 1945.

Missouri Air Force flight demonstration, September 2, 1945.